Spread the Flame

Missions Education in the Local Church

David A. Womack

Developed and Edited by the
National Sunday School Promotion and Training Department

Gospel Publishing House
Springfield, Missouri

02–0687

Library of Congress Catalog Number 92–75953
International Standard Book Number 0–88243–687–2

Printed in the United States of America

Contents

Preface

The Church is the body of Christ, in which doctrine is its brain, missions its heart, prayer its knees, and spreading the gospel its feet. Since God so loved the world that He gave His only begotten Son, missions is at the very heart of God and of His church.

The Church's missionary heart pumps human and financial resources out through its well-organized arteries to carry the life-giving gospel to the capillaries of the nations and to every cell where that gospel is being preached and applied to a God-hungry world. Then, like the depleted blood that is brought through the veins back to the heart and lungs for restoration and recharging, the missionaries are brought home for renewal and sent back out again bearing the products of the love of the Body.

That is the essence of world missions. Other facets include organization, administration, and the gigantic task of educating each new generation about the importance and methods of missions. It is the latter challenge that is the subject of this book—missions education in the local church.

In this book I am expressing two major concerns about Pentecostal churches. First, can we maintain the vision for world missions long enough to significantly fulfill our task? If we look at what has been done and what our people are doing today, we might reply affirmatively; however, our future will not depend on the past or present but on what the next generation will do. Therefore, we face a major challenge of teaching the next generation of missionaries and missions-supporting people. That is the reason for this book on missions education in the local church.

My second concern is about the quality of world evangelization. We began our task in the flaming fires of the Pentecostal revival and sent fiery-eyed and often fanatical missionaries to the four corners of the earth. They didn't always know what to do or how to do it, but they started a lot of fires that are still burning brightly today. Now with a better educated, better prepared, and more program-oriented missionary force, can we maintain the fire?

Many of the churches in which future missionaries are being raised today have little similarity to the on-fire, all-out congregations that first spread their fires by sending out missionaries as flaming torches to light up the darkness. If we are to continue what we started out to do, we must have a new outpouring of the Holy Spirit on American churches. It is in the burning hearts of local pastors and their people that fires are set that will ignite the world. This, too, is a part of missions education in the local church and the reason for the title, *Spread the Flame!*

I want to thank Glen Percifield of the Sunday School Promotion and Training Department for his patience with a busy pastor; my wife, Barbara, for putting up with all my hours at the computer; the congregation of Twin Palms Assembly of God in San Jose, California, for putting up with a pastor who was "with book"; and all the people in the Assemblies of God national offices who were so helpful.

This book is about the most important subject in the world. May you become as inspired reading it as I was writing it.

1
Lift Up Your Eyes

When you were a child, your world was only slightly bigger than you were. At first, it was hardly more than your crib, your mother's arms, your father's voice, and the faces of family, friends, and relatives. By now you have forgotten the day you discovered your own toes, but at the time it was a wonderful breakthrough that entertained you for hours on end. Of course, it probably was easier to touch your toes in those days.

When you learned to crawl, an exciting new world opened up to you; and when you began to walk, the whole house became a marvelous place of things to do and places to explore.

And then one day you found the windows. You pressed your little nose against the glass and saw another world beyond the limits of your enclosed life. When at last you were introduced to the great outdoors, your parents told you to stay in your yard; and only later were you permitted to play on your block but not to cross any streets. Then came the big day when you first went to school and entered a much larger world of classrooms, playgrounds, and friends. As you grew older, your world got larger day by day; and at last you left to seek your fortune in the even greater world of college, marriage, and work.

A big world still exists outside your windows and beyond your doors. It does not end with places to go or people to see, for there is a vast universe beyond your personal sphere to be discovered, experienced, and influenced.

The apostle Paul, writing about maturing from limited knowledge on earth to perfect knowledge in heaven, says, "When I was a child, I spake as a child, I understood as a child, I thought as a child: but when I became a man, I put away childish things" (1 Corinthians 13:11). Every growing person must experience that progressive process; we must crawl before we can walk, and walk before we can run.

The principle of physical, mental, and experiential growth may apply to anyone anywhere and at any time. However, as church people we have a special interest in this developmental process, since we face the dual challenge of (1) leading our children to personal salvation and commitment to Jesus Christ as Savior and Lord, and (2) leading believers into an understanding of and wholehearted dedication to the mission of Jesus Christ in the world. We must do more than get our children saved; we must acquaint them with the cause of Christ and produce the next generation of preachers, teachers, evangelists, prophets, and missionaries.

What we are talking about is missions education in the *local church*—everything that we do to motivate and involve people in the cause of Christ in the world and to pass down the church's mission from one generation to another.

Our Worldwide Community

Missions education is not a phrase that occurs naturally in most conversations. Although as Pentecostal believers we are among the most missions-minded Christians in the world, our idea of missions often focuses on the bravery and dedication of individual missionaries and well-publicized projects and appeals rather than on missions as a whole. In today's worldwide community, we often know the *where* or *who* of world missions, but we seldom know the *how* or *why.* Herein lies the challenge of missions education: to lead people into an understanding of and participation in the fulfillment of the Great Commission—"Go ye into all the world, and preach the gospel to every creature" (Mark 16:15).

While our personal world has been growing larger, the world itself has been shrinking. Missionaries used to travel for weeks on steamships to arrive at the lands of their calling, but today jet airplanes carry them to their fields in a few culture-shocking hours. The telephone, the telegraph, the television, and a range of telecommunications from radio to fiber optics to lasers to microwaves to orbiting satellites have combined to bring all the world within instantaneous earshot of the gospel.

National barriers are breaking down and the world is truly becoming one global village. Furthermore, the task of language learning is getting smaller. There are some 7,000 languages on earth, but most people now speak one or more of a few international tongues, such as English, Spanish, French, Portuguese, Chinese, Russian, Swahili, Hindi, and Arabic. The task still is not easy, but the goal of world evangelization seems much more attainable than in the past. The church of Jesus Christ now has more willing people with greater access to more effective resources than at any other time in its history.

Yet, while the world is getting smaller the task of world evangelization is getting bigger! In the first century when Jesus gave us the Great Commission, the world's population was about 300 million people; and it was not until Columbus discovered America that the population reached 500 million. It took just over three more centuries before 1 billion people were alive at one time. Then, the population doubled in just over 100 years to 2 billion people. From the early Depression until about 1960, we added another billion; and then we added yet another billion in the 1970s, followed by still another in the 1980s. Now, with nearly 6 billion people in the world and the projection of 7 billion by the year 2000, we confront the awesome challenge of a world out of control, destroying itself and its environment, and with limited resources to feed its masses and sustain any acceptable quality of life. That is our mission field!

How providential that just as the Great Commission was about to be out of our reach, God gave us the technology to multiply and accelerate our evangelistic efforts. But the use of those resources and the development of creative concepts to apply them to our task will require a great increase in Christian awareness and commitment. If ever we needed effective missions education, we need it today.

That brings up the question, If we are to face the urgent challenge of motivating and teaching our people to reach the world for Christ, where may we best accomplish our task of missions education?

The answer is obvious: *The most effective agency for missions education is the local church.* Where else do we have the opportunity to shape the lives of people from the cradle to the grave? What other institution so deeply affects the lives, attitudes, and choices of Christian people as the local church? Mission boards and missionary societies may employ a wide variety of educational methods and promotional means, but all will fail without a strong identification with local churches and their deep relationships and influences.

How should we respond to the call to world missions, with the heart or with the head? Is personal commitment to the cause of Jesus Christ an emotional choice or an intellectual decision? It is both and more! We respond to the missionary call with the heart and the head and the feet and the hands and the mouth—indeed, with a total dedication that gives all we are and ever hope to be to the service of our Lord and Savior Jesus Christ.

Pass It On!

We have seen the why of missions education. Now let us seek the how. How may a local church educate its people for world missions? The Bible says, "Train up a child in the way he should go: and when he is old, he will not depart from it" (Proverbs 22:6). Notice the subjects in this verse:

EDUCATION	Train up a child
DIRECTION	The way he should go
MATURATION	When he is old (or older)
CONTINUATION	He will not depart from it

Missions education must begin with the earliest impressions in childhood and continue through every phase and facet of life. The task of missions is the duty of the entire church, and we carry out that task by motivating an informed and committed congregation to teach its children, to support home and foreign missionaries, and to send forth its young people into full-time Christian service.

The Bible is absolutely clear about the church's responsibility to pass on the faith and its obligations to the next generation.

> I know him [Abraham], that he will command his children and his household after him, and they shall keep the way of the Lord, to do justice and judgment (Genesis 18:19).

> Only take heed to thyself, and keep thy soul diligently, lest thou forget the things which thine eyes have seen, and lest they depart from thy heart all the days of thy life: but teach them thy sons, and thy sons' sons (Deuteronomy 4:9).

> Thou shalt teach them diligently unto thy children, and shalt talk of them when thou sittest in thine house, and when thou walkest by the way, and when thou liest down, and when thou risest up (Deuteronomy 6:7).

> I will open my mouth in a parable: I will utter dark sayings of old: which we have heard and known, and our fathers have told us. We will not hide them from their children, showing to the generation to come the praises of the Lord, and his strength, and his wonderful works that he hath done. For he established a testimony in Jacob, and appointed a law in Israel, which he commanded our fathers, that they should make them known to their children: that the generation to come might know them, even the children which should be born; who should arise and declare them to their children: that they might set their hope in God, and not forget the works of God, but keep his commandments (Psalm 78:2–7).

> Ye fathers, provoke not your children to wrath: but bring them up in the nurture and admonition of the Lord (Ephesians 6:4).

> Continue thou [Timothy] in the things which thou hast learned and hast been assured of, knowing of whom thou hast learned them; and that from a child thou hast known the holy Scriptures, which are able to make thee wise unto salvation through faith which is in Christ Jesus (2 Timothy 3:14,15).

If, as we have said, the local church is the central agency of missions education, then why does the Bible place the responsibility on godly parents? Throughout its holy pages, God's Word emphasizes individual responsibility and faithfulness. Every family certainly educates its children by word and deed; but beyond this, in the local church Christian families combine their efforts to teach and provide role models in an organized way. The church is a community of Christian families and single believers who join forces to accomplish together what God requires of them as families and individuals.

At first glance, we might have thought that missions education was simply one of many duties in the local church, but now we see that it is at the very heart of our whole obligation for passing on the faith to the next generation and reaching out to evangelize the present generation. Missions education is a vital ministry of the whole local church.

The Urgency of the Harvest

How may we educate our people, young and old alike, about the church's task of world evangelization? How may we thrust in the sickle and reap the harvest? Jesus gave us the answers to those questions.

According to Jesus, missionary vision results from seeing the world through God's eyes. He said in John 4:35, "Say not ye, There are yet four months, and then cometh harvest? behold, I say unto you, Lift up your eyes, and look on the fields; for they are white already to harvest."

As He spoke with His disciples, Jesus compared the church's task to farmers expecting to reap a harvest. Yet He immediately pointed out that the work of the church is different from the work of the reapers of grain because there are no seasons to the worldwide harvest of souls. Farmers may say, "There are yet four months, and then cometh harvest," but the human fields in which we labor are always ripe or "white already to harvest." Therefore, the church always works in a dynamic present moment in which a harvest unreaped is grain forever lost.

Although we must plan for the future to have the people and resources to accomplish the task, we must always live and work in a vital *now* to bring in the present harvest. The apostle Paul wrote, "Now is the accepted time; behold, now is the day of salvation" (2 Corinthians 6:2). It is always the right time to spread the gospel of Jesus Christ.

Why then did Jesus use the illustration of the whitened harvest fields? When the fields are ripe and ready, farmers put everything else aside to give their whole attention to the gathering of the harvest. Jesus said the harvest of souls is ready now, and He expects His laborers to rush out to the fields, thrust in their sickles, and reap the ripened grain.

The challenge for missions education in the local church is to make people of all ages aware of the harvest fields and to inspire and motivate them to commit themselves to the demands of the harvest.

Lifted Eyes

Jesus said, "Lift up your eyes." Let's be certain we know what He meant. The New International Version of the Bible says, "Open your eyes." The New Revised Standard Version says, "Look around you." As in many passages, it turns out the King James Version is the most accurate translation of the original Greek text in which John wrote his Gospel. Generally today, people do not read as much as in previous generations, so they seek simplified and easy-to-read Bibles written in a style not found in the original Hebrew or Greek texts. No words for "open," "look," or "around you" appear in the text. Rather, John wrote the Greek word *eparate* (eh-PAH-rah-tay), a command form of a verb that meant to lift up, raise, or elevate. In different contexts it could be used to mean lift up your eyes, raise your voice, or lift up your hands in prayer.

Remember that Jesus was talking about the worldwide harvest of souls, the Great Commission or main task of the church. By saying, "Lift up your eyes," He meant we are to make a conscious effort to relate ourselves to His harvest fields. We are to become aware of the spiritual condition of a lost world and to relate ourselves to the task of reaping in the waiting fields. We must become aware of the harvest, of the urgency of the Great Commission, of the need to thrust in the sickle of world evangelism and gather in the sheaves of the Lord's golden grain. An old hymn says it very well: "Bringing in the sheaves, bringing in the sheaves, / We shall come rejoicing, bringing in the sheaves."

By saying, "Lift up your eyes," Jesus was telling us to give this subject our personal attention and purposely direct our interest to world missions. It is a command! All Christians are ordered to make the salvation of the lost a priority in their lives.

Ripe Fields

Jesus went on to say, "Look on the fields." Most translations use the English word *look* in this phrase, but the Greek word *theasasthe* (thay-AH-sas-thay) includes more than that. It means to gaze, to discern with the eyes, or to give one's full attention to something. The New Revised Standard Version says, "See how the fields are ripe for harvesting." We are to do more than look; we are to give the Lord's ripened fields our full attention! We must study, analyze, and reap the harvest.

According to the King James Version, Jesus then said that the fields "are white already to harvest." Actually, the word "already" belongs with the following sentence, so this phrase should be translated, "Because they are white to the harvest," followed by, "Already the reaper is receiving wages and gathers fruit for eternal life, that the sower and the reaper may rejoice together" (John 4:36, author's translation).

There are two activities related to the harvest: sowing and reaping. We must always be grateful for those who have gone before us to prepare the fields for today's bountiful harvest; those devoted sowers and today's faithful reapers will rejoice together in heaven over the results of their labors. But there is more! Those who reap in the Lord's harvest of souls not only are gathering fruit for life in eternity, but also are benefiting now from God's blessings. We have heard it said that God blesses a missionary-minded church. He also blesses people who become aware of the need, give it their full attention, and commit themselves to the task.

How ready is the harvest? When it comes to grain, we can say, "In 4 months comes the harvest," because a whole field is planted in one operation, grows in predictable seasons, and turns ripe at the same time. Therefore the reapers may rest and wait for the precise time to go into the fields. But not so with the Lord's harvest. New people are born every day, each one matures in his or her own lifetime, and people die every moment of every day. There is no season to God's harvest, so the reapers cannot afford to wait or say that in 4 months they will launch a single effort. It is a constantly ripe field in which every believer must labor continuously.

Let's try our own translation of Jesus' words: "Don't you say, 'Yet 4 months and the harvest comes'? Behold, I tell you, lift up your eyes and gaze intently on the fields because they are ripened white for the harvest."

Lord of the Harvest

Matthew 9:37,38 says, "Then saith he unto his disciples, The harvest truly is plenteous, but the laborers are few; pray ye therefore the Lord of the harvest, that he will send forth laborers into his harvest."

Responsible Disciples Required

First, notice that those who are to consider the harvest are Jesus' own disciples. This message is delivered directly to those who believe in Him. They are the ones responsible for personal witnessing, local evangelism, and home and foreign missions.

Awesome Harvest Awaiting

Second, there is an awesome and plentiful harvest. If Jesus could say what He did when there were only 300 million people on the earth, what must He think of today's nearly 6 billion souls—at least half of whom have not heard enough about the gospel to accept Jesus Christ as Savior and Lord? Fortunately, it is *His* harvest. He is Lord of the harvest, and we are His disciples.

Sociable Laborers Sought

Third, there is a shortage of laborers. This is one of the saddest verses in the Bible, for the harvest is great and the laborers few. As if the numbers of lost people were not enough to inspire us to urgency, the failure of most Christians to grab a sickle and go to work is disturbing. It shows a lack of understanding of what Christ and His church are all about. The simple fact is that with the present number of workers and the size of the harvest, most people alive today are apt to go into eternity without ever having heard a clear explanation of who Jesus is or how to be saved.

What then are we to do? Should we launch a worldwide recruitment program? Should every church call together its congregation next Saturday morning and hit the streets? Should we mobilize a massive movement to knock on every door? Well, yes! However, most people are not won to the Lord through mass evangelization or blitzkrieg strategies; they come to Christ by the invitation of a friend—a method that requires the best in human relationships, social graces, and honest friendship. It would be much easier if we could evangelize the world in one fell swoop. However, except for occasional bursts to bring the gospel to the attention of the masses, the work of the Lord's harvesters must occur one scythe swath at a time, with every reaper doing his or her part and overall progress resulting from the great number of harvesters in the field.

How may we attain such a widespread involvement of Christian people committed to world evangelization? Jesus said, "Pray ye therefore the Lord of the harvest, that he will send forth laborers into his harvest" (Matthew 9:38).

Pray ye! This is a challenge to spirituality, not just an alternative to good planning or religious strategies. Such human necessities as organization, mobilization, and structured evangelization will follow once we solve our spiritual problems.

Pray ye therefore! We must pray because of the plentiful condition of the harvest and the pitiful paucity of reapers. The reason for the lack of laborers is the spiritual state of the church. Only if the salvation of the lost is at the very core of its spiritual life will a church produce enough reapers to carry out its share of the harvest.

Pray ye therefore the Lord of the harvest! It is His harvest, and He is the Harvest Master. We have said the lack of workers is a spiritual problem, and that problem centers on the lordship of Jesus Christ. If He is Lord, then we will be His disciples and do His will and His work. Once this relationship has been established, He will *send forth laborers into His harvest.* The harvest fields of lost humanity constitute the natural habitat of all true Christians. It is there that we belong and are ultimately most comfortable and best adapted. Unproductive Christianity is unnatural, uncommitted, and out of God's will.

Notice that Jesus made no mention of the fields, even though that is where we generally put most of our emphasis. Our part is to pray. Once we have our attitudes, priorities, and relationships right, the Lord of the harvest will send forth laborers into His harvest. If every local church would lead its people into an awareness of the need ("Lift up your eyes"), attention to the need ("Look on the fields"), and aggressiveness in prayer for the need ("Pray ye"), we would have no shortage of reapers.

Attitude and Atmosphere

The question is, How do we create the environment in which our people may become personally aware, practically attentive, and prayerfully aggressive in the harvest?

World missions is much more than a program. It rises out of the response of every believer in every church, because missions is a state of mind, of thinking like the Lord of the harvest because we are His disciples and have prepared ourselves with Him in prayer. On our knees before God we bring ourselves into focus with His will, and it is there that the Lord of the harvest says, "Go ye into all the world, and preach the gospel to every creature" (Mark 16:15).

The challenge of missions education is to create an atmosphere in which people will respond wholeheartedly, individually and as a congregation, to the Master's call. This is our task, what we are supposed to do and how intensely we are to become involved in it.

Throughout this book we will explore many means of missions education in the local church—what to do and how to do it. However, we will be working under a basic assumption that may or may not be valid for you and your church. We are launching ahead into this study in the belief that you are Pentecostal and that your church represents the kind of Christianity that should be spread to other parts of the world. We need to ask ourselves the question, If all churches in every nation were like mine, how long would it take to evangelize the world?

Missions-Education Priority

Our first priority for missions education must be to be the kind of church where developing young missionaries in our congregation may learn the attitudes and skills they will need on the world's mission fields. If we are to expect them to see the heathen saved, filled with the Holy Spirit, healed, and delivered by the supernatural power of God, then we must train them by exposure to the same spiritual phenomena in their home churches. In the chapters that follow, we will assume that churches that want missionaries to spread the flame to the nations will themselves have that fire burning brightly in their own congregations.

2
The Great Omission

Picture a field of golden grain stretching out to the horizon, and then imagine that beyond that field there are other fields with more grain. Go even farther and think of more and more fields beyond those in every direction. The grain is heavy with wheat ripe for harvest, while in the sky black storm clouds are brewing, punctuated by lightning and echoing with distant thunder.

You are moved with a sense of urgency because the fields are ready for harvest, the time is short, and you don't see any laborers! Where are the harvesters?

And then you see them. Down in one corner of the nearest field, the workers are huddled together discussing the proper way to hold the sickle and swing the scythe and how far above the ground the cut should be.

And you think, *What are you people doing? Don't you know the fields are ready and the storm is coming? Grab a sickle! Reap the grain! Call to the landowner for more laborers! It's now or never for the harvest!*

This scene may be imaginary, but the crisis is real; for it accurately describes the condition of the worldwide harvest of human souls. Jesus said this would happen: "The harvest truly is plenteous, but the laborers are few; pray ye therefore the Lord of the harvest, that he will send forth laborers into his harvest" (Matthew 9:37,38).

Charity or Church Planting?

The Western culture has a terrible flaw. For some twisted

reason buried deeply in our past, we believe that if we have talked about a thing then we have done something about it. We are perfectly capable of providing hundreds of thousands of dollars for a research project on the state of homeless people and then finishing our task by publishing a report, while millions of shivering people still sleep in doorways with newspapers for blankets.

This problem is particularly prevalent in churches where the pastor preaches on the lostness of the heathen, the congregation celebrates its worldwide accomplishments with an annual missions convention, and missionary speakers frequently grace the pulpit; and yet the amount actually given to reach the lost is such a paltry portion of the church's total budget that the congregation's insincerity and hypocrisy are shamefully revealed. "Busy-ness" is confused with what Jesus called the "Father's business."

What exactly is the church's task? Church organizations and churchgoers differ on what they consider to be the church's main purpose. If we see the Great Commission as calling for social and economic change, then the church's emissaries will promote and perhaps even agitate for political reform or revolution. If the Great Commission points to charitable solutions in which the rich and powerful countries reach down to alleviate the poorer, the sicker, and the more suffering masses, then the church's emphasis will be on hospitals, orphanages, and distribution of goods and money. Evangelical churches view the Great Commission as a command to preach the gospel of Jesus Christ to every person on the face of the earth, so their missionary efforts center on making Christian converts, assimilating them into viable churches, and training national and international workers for even more effective evangelization in the future.

A major problem faces every Western missionary. Our civilization has given the Lord a wonderful financial and personnel pool from which to carry out the Great Commission. Surely, God must be very proud of us! Yet, the believers of the "Christian" nations must cause God both consternation and anger, for we have a bad habit of confusing evangelization with westernization. Because ours are some of the world's richest nations, many of our *converts* are reaching more for a new economic status than for eternal salvation. We tend to confuse goods with the gospel, reform with redemption, and external culture with internal conversion. We tend to be shallow in what we consider conversion to Christ. We don't recognize that such a change need not include Western clothing, middle-class values, or eating with a knife and fork manipulated in the proper hands.

A key difference between churches is their worldview and particularly their vision of how the world will end. If we think that every day in every way the world is getting better and better, finally to culminate in a wonderful utopia or man-made millennium, then our efforts will be on reform and relief to leave this world a little better than we found it. If, however, we think that Christ will soon return to catch away His church, pour out His judgment on a sinful world, and later come back with His saints to set up His own millennial reign, then we will shout salvation from the housetops, seek to save the lost from God's judgment, and consider any relief efforts as only temporary measures to ease human suffering and give credence to the primary task of evangelization.

Pentecostal churches are in the latter group, although the amazing fact is that with growing numbers of Pentecostals in the world, we may end up doing more for reform and relief than those churches that have made social action and benevolent works their major concerns. When the church emphasizes evangelism and church planting, it tends also to back up its primary efforts with a wide range of supportive ministries. We must recognize that the gospel elevates people out of despair and into hope and human dignity. If the world were to accept the gospel, many of its social, economic, and health needs would be alleviated. The old hymn is still true: "He will bring joy and gladness, take away sin and sadness; / What the world needs is Jesus, just a glimpse of Him."

Let us differentiate between *evangelism* and *evangelization.*

These two words derive from the same New Testament word that means "good news" and usually is translated "gospel." The Greek word is *euaggelion* (you-an-GHEL-ee-an). From this word we get the verb *evangelize,* to spread the gospel or to win converts to Christ. *Evangelism* and *evangelization* are nouns that describe the action of winning souls to the Lord. Yet, there is a basic difference. There have been conferences, councils, seminars, courses, books, and magazine articles on evangelism because it is the general subject of spreading the gospel, while evangelization is the act of doing it. One is talking about it; the other is doing it!

The Great Commission

The whole question of the church's purpose centers on what Jesus meant when He gave the Great Commission—His command to take the good news of salvation to every person on the face of the earth. What we call the Great Commission is stated in various Scripture passages, each with its important elements.

In Matthew 28:18–20, Jesus said,

> All power is given unto me in heaven and in earth. Go ye therefore, and teach all nations, baptizing them in the name of the Father, and of the Son, and of the Holy Ghost: teaching them to observe all things whatsoever I have commanded you: and, lo, I am with you alway, even unto the end of the world.

In this passage, the King James Version does not give us a full understanding of the original text. There are various Greek words for "power," and this one means "authority." For example, your car's engine gives you the power to drive the vehicle, but your driver's license gives you the authority to do so. Jesus has been given all authority. Therefore, based on His authority, the church may carry out its divine task.

Two more words in the passage need explanation: "teach" and "teaching," translations of two different Greek words. The first means to make disciples or converts, and the second means to instruct or to teach. Christians are to go forth and make disciples or converts of all peoples. We are to follow up our convert-making by assimilating the new disciples into the church by baptizing them in the name of the Father, Son, and Holy Spirit. Having done that, we are to continue to teach the new Christians to obey all Christ's commandments. There is no hint here of indiscriminate evangelism without gathering the converts into established churches. Rather, every person discipled for Christ is to be baptized according to Jesus' trinitarian formula and brought into a full relationship with the church.

The short-term goal of getting people to accept Christ must be followed by the intermediate goal of baptizing new converts, resulting in the long-term goal of bringing believers into full obedience to all the teachings of Christ. Evangelization must be followed by assimilation and education. This cycle results in further evangelization and an ever-expanding continuation of the cycle.

AN EVER-EXPANDING CYCLE OF EVANGELISM	
EVANGELIZATION	Witnessing & Convert-Making
ASSIMILATION	Incorporation Into the Church
EDUCATION	Teaching and Development
GREATER EVANGELIZATION, ASSIMILATION, & EDUCATION	
EVEN GREATER EVANGELIZATION . . .	

In Mark 16:15, Jesus said, "Go ye into all the world, and preach the gospel to every creature." In this presentation of the Great Commission, we are told how to start, where to go, what to do when we get there, and to whom we are to deliver the message. No one could possibly misunderstand Jesus' command. Therefore, any Christian who is not involved in the propagation of the gospel is disobedient to Christ!

Jesus went on to say, "He that believeth and is baptized shall be saved; but he that believeth not shall be damned" (verse 16). Whether people will be saved or lost is up to us. If they believe the gospel and are assimilated into the church, they will be saved; but if they do not believe, or if we fail to tell them, they will be lost.

Baptism

We have seen two passages in which Jesus told us to baptize the converts that result from our evangelization. To these statements we can add Peter's words on the Day of Pentecost: "Repent, and be baptized every one of you . . . and ye shall receive the gift of the Holy Ghost" (Acts 2:38).

Water baptism basically is a personal identification with Jesus Christ's death and resurrection. Through baptism we follow the example and commandments of our Lord. Baptism is an important step in assimilating new converts into the church. It should be one of the first actions of the new believer. Baptism does not save us, for we are saved by the blood of Jesus; but it is an act that is required of every saved believer. Although it is theoretically possible for someone who never had the opportunity to be baptized to be saved (such as people who get saved on their deathbed or while going down in a falling airplane), all those who do have the opportunity are supposed to be baptized. Peter said, "Every one of you." The real question is not whether or not to be baptized but whether or not to be a Christian.

Signs and Wonders

Jesus then promised to back up His evangelizing believers with supernatural signs (Mark 16:17,18). In the name of Jesus, they would cast out devils and speak with new tongues, they would pick up serpents with their hands or drink deadly poison and it would not hurt them, and they would lay hands on the sick and have them recover.

Jesus promised these supernatural miracles to all believers who would go into the whole world and proclaim the gospel to all people. If our Lord himself felt He must rely on signs and wonders to carry out His ministry and promised the same powers to His followers, how then can any church hope to fulfill its task today without God's supernatural power at work in its services and ministries? The doctrine of God's infinite love and power requires us to believe in healing, deliverance, and answered prayer. Simply put, our God can and will do anything consistent with His nature to support His own cause and those who dedicate themselves to it.

Another Great Commission statement is in Luke 24:46–48:

> [Jesus] said unto them, Thus it is written, and thus it behooved Christ to suffer, and to rise from the dead the third day: and that repentance and remission of sins should be preached in his name among all nations, beginning at Jerusalem. And ye are witnesses of these things.

In this passage Jesus gave a more detailed description of the gospel we are to preach. The Greek word translated "Christ" means the *Anointed One,* the Hebrew word *Messiah.* Jesus was to suffer and die on the cross and rise from the dead on the third day. This was to be the basis for preaching to all people everywhere the gospel, or good news, of "repentance and remission of sins." Because of Christ's suffering, death on the cross, and resurrection, all who repent may have their sins remitted (forgiven) and no longer held against them. As His witnesses, we are to proclaim this gospel, beginning where we first receive it and taking it to all nations.

In John 20:21, Jesus said, "As my Father hath sent me, even so send I you." Here we see who sends and who goes. Just as the Father had sent His Son into the world, Jesus would send forth His church. Inferred is the idea that we are to do what Jesus did. Our Lord said, "He that believeth on me, the works that I do shall he do also; and greater works than these shall he do; because I go unto my Father" (John 14:12). Again we are promised miraculous answers to prayer to support our evangelistic witness.

Just before Jesus ascended into heaven, He said in Acts 1:8, "Ye shall receive power, after that the Holy Ghost is come upon you: and ye shall be witnesses unto me both in Jerusalem, and in all Judea, and in Samaria, and unto the uttermost part of the earth." Like Christians today, the disciples were curious about when certain prophecies would take place. Jesus told them they were not to know the exact dates that the Father had retained in His own exclusive power (authority). Rather, they were to receive dynamic power (force or energy) when they were filled with the Holy Spirit. As a result, they would be Christ's witnesses in Jerusalem, continue outward to the surrounding region of Judea, go to the next land of Samaria, and reach out to the most remote places on earth.

Simultaneous Not Sequential Evangelism

Some have mistakenly interpreted this verse to claim that the gospel should first be preached to one's home city, then to one's nation, then to nearby countries, and finally to distant lands. The problem is the task is never done; we can't wait until Jerusalem is Christian before we go out to Judea and Samaria. Notice, however, that Jesus said the disciples would be His witnesses *both* in Jerusalem *and* in the other areas. Home and foreign missions are both important and are to be carried out simultaneously, not in sequence.

Although any one of the Great Commission Scripture passages should in itself be enough to send us into the highways and byways of the world with our Bibles in hand, we can gain a deeper understanding of our task and resources by looking at them as a whole. Because we have been sent by the Father, we are to go to all the people in every geographical place on earth and proclaim the gospel of Jesus Christ. As a result of our worldwide witness, we are to make disciples or converts of everyone we can, assimilate them into churches through Christian baptism, and follow up our initial ministries by establishing stable churches with vibrant Sunday schools where we may continue to teach believers to observe all the teachings of Christ and to train them for further ministry.

These Scripture passages not only tell us what to do, but also tell us about the resources available to accomplish our task. Jesus gave us the wonderful promise that He will always accompany us: "Lo, I am with you alway, even unto the end of the world" (Matthew 28:20). He further promised that our worldwide witness would result from the baptism in the Holy Spirit, which would both inspire our witness and impel us to carry the gospel to the ends of the earth. Supernatural signs would be manifested wherever believers would be at work: casting out devils, speaking in other tongues, delivering from natural or man-made dangers, and healing by the laying on of hands. We have the authority to go and the power to act when we get there. Such is the Great Commission and the great condition of the Church.

Aggressive, Assertive, and Assured Evangelism

In giving the simple command to go everywhere and tell everybody, Jesus has clearly said that He intends for His church to be aggressive, assertive, and assured of success. Yet, many Christians today identify themselves with conservative churches. "Conservative Christianity" is a contradiction of terms. Born in the violence of the cross, true Christianity has always been something worth dying for. How could any born-again, Spirit-filled, heaven-bound saint of God be conservative about Jesus Christ or His gospel? If all people are sinners headed for eternal hell, and only by the blood of Jesus can they be snatched away and rescued for heaven, then it is urgent that every Christian become a fiery-eyed fanatic and passionate agitator for the cause of Christ. The servant must emulate the Master!

Do you remember when your mother would say before leaving the house, "Wash the dishes before I get back"? You would be sure to wash those dishes, because you knew the last thing she said before she left would be the first thing she would ask about when she returned. The last thing Jesus said before ascending into heaven was that Spirit-filled believers would be His witnesses all over the world; and we may be sure it will be the first thing He will ask about when He comes back. Yet, like disobedient children, many Christians have ignored the Great Commission and turned it into the Great Omission!

How very sad that just when we have the technology, the transportation, and the techniques to win the world for Christ, many Christian people, churches, and denominations are confused about the meaning of Christianity and are declining in their involvement in world evangelism. We must face the awful truth that backslidden Christians are as heathen as any pagans on earth, and that those who have failed to evangelize must now be considered among the objects of our evangelization. The old saying is true: You're either a missionary or a mission field.

World missions is not an option but a commandment. The only choice is whether or not to follow Christ. Once that decision is made, the command is, "Go!" There are no other alternatives, no other ways to be a Christian. The Great Commission calls for a great commitment.

The Three Ships

The Pentecostal movement is the fastest-growing major element in the Church today. It is a revival of the beliefs, experiences, practices, and priorities of the New Testament. Pentecostals are those who identify themselves with the Church that was born on the Day of Pentecost in A.D. 30. They believe there is one true form of Christianity—that which was founded by Jesus Christ and taught in the New Testament by His first followers. They believe the same doctrines as the New Testament believers, they have the same experiences of salvation and baptism in the Holy Spirit, they carry out the same practices of Communion and water baptism, and they treat as important the same things that were important to the first Christians.

The Pentecostal movement grew out of an outpouring of the Holy Spirit in Topeka, Kansas, in 1901, and the Azusa Street Revival in Los Angeles beginning in 1906. The Movement spread quickly in the United States and soon was sending missionaries around the world. It is represented today by a number of Pentecostal groups, the largest of which is the Assemblies of God, organized in 1914 at Hot Springs, Arkansas, for the following purposes:

1. To send out and support Pentecostal missionaries
2. To publish Pentecostal literature such as Sunday school materials, hymnals, books, and magazines
3. To develop Bible schools to train Pentecostal pastors, evangelists, and missionaries
4. To unite the Pentecostal movement in a cooperative Fellowship

The official minutes of the first meeting of the Assemblies of God in 1914 begin like this: "For a number of years, God has been leading men to seek for a full apostolic gospel standard of experience and doctrine." Those official opening words of the Assemblies of God are still the best definition of our Fellowship.

At a second meeting in Chicago in the fall of 1914, the delegates said, "We commit ourselves and the movement to Him for the greatest evangelism that the world has ever seen." Since that time, the growth of the Assemblies of God has been phenomenal in spite of wars, economic depressions, false doctrines, and the unpredictable whims of contemporary religious trends. The church grew especially fast after World War II, causing many growing congregations to expand their facilities or build new ones and to develop new programs in the 1950s and early 1960s. The changes were needed, but new and larger churches required different kinds of pastors with more administrative and social skills, and there was less tolerance for the more radical preachers of an earlier day. It was a necessary stage because some of the most earnest preachers today are also well-educated and skilled in pastoral leadership.

The world went through great changes in the 1960s. All the values of society were being questioned, and the church was under scrutiny for its relevancy in the world. The Assemblies of God came out of those times stronger than ever because they dared to ask questions about their identity and purpose. A declaration was presented at the 1968 Council on Evangelism in St. Louis, Missouri, which later was adopted by the General Council of the Assemblies of God and included in the Statement of Fundamental Truths. It was a major step forward that allowed greater breadth to the Movement and formed a stronger base for worldwide growth.

The question asked at the Council on Evangelism was, "What is the purpose of the church?" Before 1968, the reply would have been, "The purpose of the church is evangelism." But because they dared to question the very foundational concepts of the church, they were able to add great strength and stability to the Movement and prepare the way for the massive growth today.

Out of the Council on Evangelism came what is called the threefold ministry of the Church: *ministry to the Lord, ministry to the Church, and ministry to the world.*

At first glance, the Church's triple purpose may seem obvious and so simple that anyone should have been able to state it previously. Yet, the very simplicity of the concept shows the depth of thought that went into it. Another way to think about it is illustrated by the cross, which points upward to the Lord, downward to the earth, and outward to the world. The Church must minister upward to God in praise and devotion, inward to the Church in edification and care, and outward to the world in evangelism and love.

Christopher Columbus traveled to America in three Spanish ships—the *Pinta,* the *Nina,* and the *Santa Maria.* Likewise the Church moves forward in its quest in its "three ships" of worship, fellowship, and discipleship, the threefold ministry of the Church.

Thus the Assemblies of God grew into a fully developed church that provides a whole, well-rounded ministry that fulfills its obligations to God, to the congregation, and to the world. The former single purpose of evangelism was brought into proper balance and given a foundation for the stable growth in the millions that we see today.

For the local church, this calls for a balance that praises and pleases God, cares for all the needs of the congregation, and reaches out in evangelism to the unchurched. All three must be done simultaneously and with equal emphasis. If a church majors on praise alone, it will become unstable and fail to develop its people or to make converts. If it stresses the care of the congregation to the neglect of worship and evangelism, it will become little more than a social club with no converts and no sense of the presence of God. If it puts all its emphasis on evangelism, but neglects worship and congregational life, it might produce new converts but it won't know how to develop them. What we need, then, is a proper balance of worship, fellowship, and discipleship, the threefold ministry of the Church.

In Matthew 28:18–20, Jesus told us to make disciples, baptize them, assimilate them into the church, and continue to teach them all His commandments. He said He would be with us always. There it is—ministry to the Lord, ministry to the church, and ministry to the world. With this balanced and integrated approach to the whole ministry of the church, we greatly strengthen our worldwide witness for Christ.

3
Your Missions IQ

In spite of its wars and unprecedented destruction, the 20th century has been a time of great advancements. In one cataclysmic century we have gone from stagecoaches to spaceships. We wash and dry clothing and dishes in automatic machines, cook food in microwave ovens, and use computers for everything from word processing to shopping. From toothpaste to telecommunications, our lives have changed so dramatically that our daily activities and personal outlook bear little resemblance to those of our recent ancestors.

So rapidly have come the changes that only the most adaptable and best educated people can keep up with the flow of progress. Older folks around the world have found it difficult to understand the younger generations or to pass on their traditional values. Therefore, the younger generations are less rooted in their past than were any of their predecessors and are more open to the gospel.

One of the most helpful discoveries of the 20th century is a way to measure human intelligence and rate it with a number called the intelligence quotient or IQ. The average IQ is 100[1]. A few extremely disadvantaged people have an IQ as low as 40, and some especially gifted ones are over 160. But most people are somewhere in the middle range between 80 and 120. Many creative people such as writers and artists are in the 135–145 range, and most geniuses are rated at 150 or higher.

The IQ system does not always correlate with actual school grades or achievements because it cannot measure a person's motivation or opportunity to learn. Children with an average

IQ do not have to be limited to *C* grades, but with inspiration, motivation, and helpful role models can do almost anything to which they set their minds. On the other hand, high-IQ children may tend to put things off until the last minute and fail to fulfill their potential for higher grades.

While missions intelligence is different from mental intelligence, increasing our understanding of missionaries and our role in missions can help us to better accomplish God's purpose for our world.

A few years ago when the Division of Foreign Missions was giving a language-aptitude test to missionary candidates it was not unusual to find that less than half of them had high language-learning skills. Yet, the results a few years later showed that many of the high-aptitude people had failed to learn a language well, while others who had tested poorly had become fluent. What was missing in the test was a measure of the candidates' motivation and their desire to learn the language and to share the gospel of Jesus Christ with others. Also, missionaries who must trust God for so many other things find that God helps them. Speaking in other tongues is not the ability to learn another language, yet Spirit-filled people have access to miraculous levels of language learning.

In missions education, we must remember that the people we seek to influence represent a wide range of intelligence and learning abilities. Churches possess a greater variety of motivational and learning tools than most other teaching institutions and can successfully communicate their missionary cause. We must remember, too, that anyone can work for God; it takes all kinds of people to reach all kinds of people.

Consider what the people in your church know or don't know about their world. What would happen if next Sunday you were to give a test to everyone in your Sunday school class? On a single page you would have a line drawing of the continents and major islands of the western hemisphere. How many people could correctly identify more than 10 countries? If you want to get really discouraged about what people know about their world, try having them identify the states on a map of the United States!

This leads to the question, How much do our people really know about world missions?

A Self Test

When we ask how much our people know about missions, we are faced with other vital questions. In fact, a church's ability and opportunity to ask questions about its own ministries are signs of congregational health.

1. *How may we know if our church truly is missions-minded?*

We may be tempted to compare our missions performance with that of other congregations. Are we listed among our district's top missions-giving churches? Do we have a display case filled with trophies and plaques extolling our accomplishments? Certainly it is commendable to excel at missions giving, but our task is much greater than may ever be measured by money. Jesus once complimented a widow for giving two small coins, even though other donors had given much more money. The reason for this apparent discrepancy was that she had given all she had, while others had given only a portion. Perhaps we should measure missions giving not by what we give but by what we have left!

Three things are required of every congregation that wants to be missions-minded: (1) to support the work of foreign and home missionaries with adequate funds; (2) to pray effectively for the missionaries and their work; and (3) to educate, motivate, and inspire the congregation so that they will respond to the call to world missions.

2. *Is our church's missions program an adequate response to world needs?*

This question is impossible to answer. What do we mean by "adequate"? The word itself is inadequate because it infers doing a minimum for missions, whereas the whole spirit of world evangelism is to do all we can for Christ. The other problem with this question is that fewer than half of the nearly 6 billion people in the world have received a clear enough witness to know how to accept Jesus Christ as Savior and Lord. Success at world evangelism cannot be measured by the programs of local churches; it must involve a cooperative effort by a large number of participating congregations.

3. *How much missions emphasis is enough?*

To that question we ask, "Enough for what?" As we have discussed, like the upward, downward, and outward directions of the cross, the church has a threefold ministry—upward to God, inward to the church, and outward to the world. Rather than thinking in terms of what is barely enough, we must seek a stable relationship between the "three ships" of worship, fellowship, and discipleship. A healthy interaction should exist between giving the Lord praise, giving the congregation love and care, and giving the world the gospel of Jesus Christ.

4. *Shouldn't there be a balance between missions and the other programs of the church?*

Surprisingly, the answer is no! World missions is not simply another program but a necessary element of all church ministries. Much as sugar pervades the whole cake rather than being concentrated in one part, missions must permeate and flavor the entire church. The Sunday school has the Boys and Girls Missionary Crusade (BGMC) to provide Christian education materials for missionaries. The Men's Ministries has the Light–for–the–Lost (LFTL) ministry to provide missionaries with evangelistic literature. Youth Ministries has the Speed–the–Light (STL) ministry to supply missionaries with automobiles and other equipment, and the Women's Ministries provides large amounts of household goods, clothing, and project money for missionaries. Every ministry in the church should have its missions feature, without limitations and without competition.

Seven Signs of a Missions-Minded Church

Many people have confirmed that God loves and blesses a missions-minded church. When we get the church behind God's ministry, He blesses our programs.

It is difficult to measure a church's missionary success, but certainly the following indications should guarantee a deep commitment to world evangelization.

1. *The congregation will hear frequently about missions and missionaries.*

Most churches committed to missions have 10 or more missionary guest speakers each year, and many have 1 each month. There is no ideal number, only that a church should see and hear missionaries often enough to be profoundly and positively influenced by them and their divine cause. Please remember to include the children in the sanctuary service or ask the missionary to visit children's church.

2. *Missionary speakers will often be featured in the main services.*

Pastors show their congregations what is important by what they feature in their services. Although a few missionaries may not be skilled Sunday morning speakers, many will be among the best preachers the people will hear. The Sunday morning services of most growing churches are built around the preaching of the pastor, so many pastors schedule missionaries for a part of the service and then bring a short pastoral message. It is better to expose a lot of people to 20 minutes of missions than to give a missionary the whole service for fewer people in a midweek service.

3. *Church attendance will not decline when there is a missionary speaker or other missions emphasis.*

Attendance may go down for missionary services because some churchgoers will avoid what they perceive as fund-raising for a program. A church can avoid this by proper missions education, teaching its people that missionary speakers relate the church to the greater picture of what God is doing in the world and exposing young people to role models for higher Christian service. And, of course, missionaries do have the obvious need for financial and prayer support. Well-attended missionary services are a clear sign of a missions-minded church.

4. *The church will support missionaries and missions projects financially.*

Money is essential to world evangelization, just as it is for the local church. Almost everything related to world missions costs money—airfares, housing, household furnishings, utilities, automobile maintenance, children's schooling, language learning, travel, literature, church construction, Bible schools, medical expenses, and much more. We don't give missionaries money because they beg for it, but because it is our way of sending them out to accomplish our mutual worldwide calling. By having missionaries itinerate among churches to raise support, we expose churches to their influence and allow ourselves to respond to individual missionaries. Don't feel too sorry for itinerating missionaries as they endeavor to raise support before leaving for their fields; churches, too, must raise their budgets every week. Ministering in many churches over 12 to 18 months is excellent experience for a missionary candidate; he or she goes from a local pastorate to a national ministry. When veteran missionaries return after a term overseas, itineration among churches renews the motivation that first sent them out to the harvest fields.

5. *Missions will pervade the whole church rather than be limited to certain departments.*

Some churches have a reputation for their support of a departmental missions emphasis, but the congregation's missions ministry will be strongest if it pervades the church's whole range of age-levels. Churches need to catch the vision of what the departmental programs are intended to do. Through the Boys and Girls Missionary Crusade we teach our children to recognize and care for the lost and to give to missions so the lost may be saved. Through Speed–the–Light we teach our young people to be personally involved in supporting world-evangelism missions and to surrender their lives to Christ for His worldwide harvest. And through Light–for–the–Lost and Women's Ministries we involve adults in special missionary projects. All these missions endeavors are supplemental to the basic foundation of monthly missionary support.

6. *There will be organized and individual prayer for missionaries and their work.*

The evangelization of the world is a spiritual response to a divine calling. A special partnership exists between home or foreign missionaries, the people who support them, and those who pray. This bonding is unlike any other teamwork in the world; for each requires the other, and together they work miracles. People who have learned the blessing of prayer for missionaries have little interest in prayers that end, "And bless all the missionaries. Amen." Effective missionary prayer is specific prayer that names people, places, and projects before the Lord and often intercedes until the answer comes.

7. *Young people and others from the church will be called into missionary service.*

A church has not given enough for missions until it has placed its own sons and daughters in the offering. A missions-minded church will produce after its own kind. It will go beyond exposing its young people to missionary speakers by involving its youth in local evangelization and missions projects. Many churches send their young people on short-term evangelism trips with Ambassadors in Mission (AIM) or longer-term service such as with the Division of Foreign Missions, *Missions Abroad and Placement Service* (MAPS–DFM), and the Division of Home Missions, *Missions America Placement Service* (MAPS–DHM).

Just one of these seven signs doesn't necessarily indicate a truly missions-minded church, but the combination of all seven will certainly guarantee it.

A Foreign Education

As we have seen, missions involvement is a spiritual commitment. Yet, the more we know about missions and the world the more specific may be our response in giving, praying, and yielding to God's call.

Geography

Anyone who wants to pray meaningfully for missions should have a working knowledge of the world globe. One missionary asked a congregation, "Has anyone here ever prayed for Gambia?" No one had heard of it, much less prayed! Gambia is a small West African country on both banks of the Gambia River and mostly surrounded by the nation of Senegal. There are dozens of countries that few of our people would recognize.

Many people cannot even name the continents. One church member asked a missionary to Costa Rica to take his greetings to a missionary in Argentina—a quarter of a world away! A standard story among missionaries is that of the barrel of used tea bags reportedly shipped to missionaries in India. It might have helped if the donor had known that the tea had come from India in the first place. Yes, we'd better learn some geography!

The world is not exactly round like a ball but shaped more like a pumpkin with both ends slightly flattened and somewhat fattened at the middle. It is surrounded at the waist, so to speak, by the equator, an imaginary line that encircles the globe—not to be confused with the "menagerie lion that runs around the earth," as one child understood it.

Much of the earth is covered by water, a fact all too real to the early missionaries who sailed the seas for weeks to arrive at their fields. Sailors talk of the Seven Seas—the Atlantic Ocean, the Pacific Ocean, the Mediterranean Sea, the Indian Ocean, the Caribbean Sea, the Arctic Ocean, and the Antarctic Ocean—or some such combinations of oceans and seas.

Similarly, there are seven continents: North America, South America, Europe, Asia, Africa, Australia, and Antarctica. These land masses do not quite account for such areas as Central

America, the Caribbean, the Pacific Islands, Iceland, or Greenland.

The Assemblies of God has its mission fields divided into home and foreign missions.

The Division of Home Missions is focused on reaching the American mission field through its six departments. *New Church Evangelism* is concerned with planting new churches to reach our country with the gospel. *Chi Alpha Campus Ministries* places missionaries on secular college and university campuses. *Teen Challenge* reaches and disciples those being destroyed by life-controlling problems. The *Chaplaincy Department* covers industrial and institutional chaplains as well as military chaplains. *Intercultural Ministries* reaches the culturally diverse, as well as the deaf, blind, and those with other handicaps. *MAPS/RV: Mission America Placement Service* coordinates lay volunteers who utilize their trade or other skills in local churches needing short-term help.

Foreign missions ministry has four fields, each led by a field director: Africa, Eurasia (Europe, the Middle East, and Southern Asia), the Asia Pacific (the Orient and the Pacific Islands), and Latin America and the Caribbean. Some foreign countries have their own similar Pentecostal churches, so we do not usually send missionaries to Canada, Great Britain, the Scandinavian countries, Australia, or New Zealand, although we maintain good relationships with our sister organizations in those countries.

Cultures and Languages

The world in which our foreign missionaries live and work is a complex network, different everywhere yet interrelated in a single global system. The old world is gone, and in its place is a new world bound together by trade, telecommunications, telephones, and treaties. Many primitive huts have transistor radios daily linking them to the world.

Some factors are basic to missions everywhere, but every field is unique. Countries are like people; there is a broad range of upper, middle, and lower classes.

IF 150 COUNTRIES WERE PEOPLE . . .	
5 Upper Class	Advanced and independently wealthy landowners
10 Upper-Middle Class	Entrepreneurs, moderately well-off but taking risks
35 Middle Class	Living well with hard work, educated, but salaried by the above groups
50 Lower-Middle Class	Subsistence level, in debt, poorly prepared, doing menial jobs
30 Upper-Lower Class	Poor but economically stable, living in traditional roles with little modern technology
20 Lower-Lower Class	Critically underdeveloped and dependent on others

Besides the variety of economic conditions in mission-field countries, language problems present difficulties to those whose task it is to communicate the gospel. Language differences have been part of the gospel challenge since the Day of Pentecost. Most missionaries continue to name overcoming language barriers as the biggest problem of their ministry.

Some missionaries work in English-speaking areas, but most must learn one of the international languages, such as Spanish, French, Portuguese, Arabic, or Swahili. Others learn single-nation languages, such as German, Italian, Hebrew, Hindi, Japanese, or Tagalog. Still others have to learn tribal or regional dialects, often in addition to the national tongue. Many missionaries attend some sort of language school for at least a year. But for the tribal tongues they must be trained in linguistics and phonetics and learn directly from native tutors. Few people in American congregations have any idea of the years of preparation that go into making these missionaries such accomplished professionals for God.

Religious Differences

Missionaries face major challenges in the realm of religion. It is precisely for this reason that God calls them to preach the gospel to other countries. Religion takes on many forms, but missionaries are confronted mostly by seven varieties.

1. *Traditional Christianity*—Pentecostals believe there is one true form of Christianity, that which was taught by Jesus Christ and passed down to us by His first followers in the New Testament. By this definition, some groups that go by the name "Christian" but have strayed from New Testament standards or blended with heathen influences may not be Christian at all, and therefore may have themselves become the objects of missionary endeavor.

2. *Islam*—A large number of people in the world are of various sects of Islam, many of them in countries we call the Bible lands. Generally, the Muslims have been so violently opposed to Christianity that work among them has been difficult. Yet, we see encouraging progress today, especially since the Persian Gulf War of 1991.

3. *Buddhism*—This Eastern belief system is more a philosophy than a religion, since it does not usually include the concept of God. There are many sects, many of which have blended with other local religions or relate to some other major religion such as China's Confucianism or Japan's Shintoism.

4. *Hinduism*—Found mostly in India or other places where Indian people have gone, Hinduism has many gods and local variations. One of its concepts is that it includes and explains all other religions. It separates people into many castes or social levels. India also has such diverse religions as Jainism, Sikhism, and the Zoroastrian Parsees.

5. *Judaism*—The religion of the Jews also has various sects. Descended from biblical Judaism, it went through some great rabbinical changes after the destruction of the temple in A.D.

70 and during the Middle Ages. Much of this ancient forerunner of Christianity today is dedicated mainly to maintaining Jewish culture and heritage.

6. *Animism*—People who believe that spirits dwell in such things as trees, animals, streams, or rocks are called animists. Animistic religion is often found among tribal people, including the American Indians and most Africans. It comes in two main varieties, those who practice sun and ancestor worship and those who turn to moon worship, the underworld, and the occult. Most witchcraft comes from the latter form or dark side of animism.

7. *Syncretism*—In all parts of the world new religions have formed out of combinations of the old. Syncretism is a merging of religious beliefs or using bits and pieces of other religions to create a new belief system. American examples would be Mormonism, Seventh-Day Adventism, Jehovah's Witnesses, and the emerging New Age Movement.

We must remember that people who come to Jesus Christ are converting from some other religion or philosophy. Missionaries must be experts in the culture and religion from which they are saving the lost.

Governments

Yet another challenge to missionaries is government. As in our other lists, there are seven kinds of government:

1. Democratic republics
2. Communistic/socialistic governments
3. Kingdoms/emirates
4. Dictatorships
5. Dependencies of other nations
6. Tribal chiefdoms
7. Revolutionary or provisional juntas

Much of what we have said about foreign missionaries applies to home missionaries who also serve under difficult circumstances.

We have seen the real world in which missionaries labor. Now perhaps we may realize what adaptable, knowledgeable, well-prepared, and intelligent people they must be to work so successfully in such a complicated world. We tend to compare them in unrealistic ways by their appearance or presentations, their speaking and musical abilities, or their mastery of materialistic values such as self-promotion, motivational skills, organizational gifts, or salesmanship.

Gifts and Aptitudes

Following are seven ways to judge the effectiveness of missionaries:

1. Personal commitment to Jesus Christ
2. Knowledge of the Bible
3. Walk in the Spirit
4. Linguistic skills
5. Intercultural communication talents
6. Quality of their Christian witness in a non-Christian environment
7. Proven record of convert-making

To this list we could add qualities such as good administration, leadership, and innovation, traits that are required of all ministers anywhere in the world.

All of us should admire and support missionaries. They are a special force of Christian ministers who leave behind their comfort zones and loved ones and give of themselves sacrificially for others' salvation.

Organization and coordination of missionary efforts, one of the original goals of the Assemblies of God, continues to receive emphasis throughout the Fellowship.

A Visit to Springfield

The International Headquarters of the General Council of the Assemblies of God is located at 1445 Boonville Avenue in

Springfield, Missouri. The original founding meeting took place in 1914 at Hot Springs, Arkansas, because it was a tourist town in the middle of the country and on a railroad line. In 1974 the Assemblies of God returned to Hot Springs to commemorate its 60th anniversary and to cooperate with the Arkansas Historical Society in laying a bronze plaque in the sidewalk in front of the site of the old Opera House where the first meetings were held.

For a short time the offices of the new Fellowship were in St. Louis, Missouri, but were moved to Springfield when someone offered some land there. It made a lot of sense at the time because the Frisco Railway went through the town and Springfield was on Route 66, the main highway across the United States. For many years the offices were at 434 West Pacific Street. The site of the present headquarters on Boonville Avenue used to be a ballfield. Today it is a whole complex of buildings spread over various sites, including the administrative offices, Gospel Publishing House, the Assemblies of God Theological Seminary, and other offices and services.

Over the years, there has been some discussion about why the offices are called the International Headquarters. Actually, it is the national headquarters for the church in the United States. However, because the Assemblies of God has administrative leadership over foreign missionaries working in many foreign countries, it is indeed international—so long as we realize that missionaries have raised up indigenous churches in every country, each with its own leadership. The worldwide Movement is held together by fraternal bonds of fellowship, not by direct administrative oversight.

Such offices are essential to administer the growing church in America with its army of home and foreign missionaries. A national office serves the same purpose as a church office. Someone has to lead the ministry, administer the funds, put out the literature, and keep the organization on course. We must not be opposed to administration, nor should we apply to the church any negative feelings that might come from our political views of government. The hundreds of people who work at headquarters are dedicated Christian ministers and laypeople who provide for us many valuable services.

If you and I could park our car in the parking lot and walk in the front door, we would be greeted by a receptionist in the lobby who would direct us to the divisions and departments we would seek. Since we are interested in missions education in the local church, we could ask about the *Boys and Girls Missionary Crusade* in the Sunday School Promotion and Training Department, *Speed–the–Light* in the Youth Department, *Light–for–the–Lost* in the Men's Ministries Department, or the *Missionary Adoption Plan* and *Etta Calhoun Fund* in the Women's Ministries Department. You would be pleased with their friendliness and willingness to help.

In the Division of Home Missions we would find people at many desks working with special ministries and church planting in America and with their promotional publications. Much of their work is in coordinating activities going on in all the districts across the country.

Down the carpeted hallway past the executive offices we would come to the Division of Foreign Missions made up of the offices of the members of the Foreign Missions Administrative Committee, including those of the foreign field directors and other leaders. We would see an editorial department, an accounting office, and many people working at networking ministries around the world.

You might wonder how such a large operation could be directed from these offices. The answer is that what happens at the International Headquarters is only the tip of the iceberg, so to speak, of a great army of dedicated ministers, lay workers, and missionaries across America and around the world who carry out the great task of world evangelization. We may be rightfully proud to be a part of such an effective Fellowship as it reaches out its arms to the whole world in love and obedience to Jesus Christ.

---

[1] *Academic American Encyclopedia.* (Danbury, Conn.: Grolier Electronic Publishing, 1992), "Intelligence," by Philip E. Vernon (Prodigy).

4
What Is a Missionary?

An itinerating missionary was taking off from Denver's Stapleton Airport in a propeller-driven commuter airplane. Soon after the plane was airborne, the pilot banked it rather sharply. The mountains seemed to rise out of view, and the passengers were looking down on streets and houses.

A little girl sitting across the aisle from the missionary said excitedly to her father, "Daddy, Daddy, the world is turning sideways!"

The father responded to his daughter, "No, honey. It's not the world, it's us."

The Bible begins with the wonderful declaration, "In the beginning God created the heaven and the earth" (Genesis 1:1). God made a beautiful world and said "it was very good" (1:31). However, soon after man's appearance, the planet lost its innocence and replaced God's good earth with a world of trouble. The very first family sinned against God, and Adam and Eve became the world's first refugees as they were driven from their original home in the Garden of Eden and forced to survive in a strange land. Women would henceforth bear the pain of childbirth, and men would have to earn their bread by the sweat of their brow. One of Adam and Eve's children, Cain, murdered his brother Abel over the issue of whose religious practices were more acceptable to God. That was how the world began!

Today we face the same critical issues that caused our ancestors to sin. Some people think the world is getting worse, but human nature has not changed in ages. It's just that there are so many more of us now, and people have learned so many more ways to hurt, tempt, or exploit one another. We still live in a fallen world in which individuals live out the same drama of falling from God, with the resulting effects of sin, for "all have sinned, and come short of the glory of God" (Romans 3:23). The most pressing problems of our world are still those faced by Adam and Eve and their family: the environment, the food supply, employment, childbearing, dishonesty, violence, and disobedience to God.

It is in this world turned sideways that missionaries are called to minister. The problems of sin were solved and resolved when Jesus Christ died on the cross, and now we may announce to the whole world the good news of salvation from sin, restoration to righteousness, and eternal life with God.

Just as today's difficulties are the same age-old challenges that have always concerned the human race, so the real answers to the world's needs are the same. At the heart of all our difficulties is the central problem of how we relate to God and live by His commandments. We may ask, "Why doesn't God do something about the world?" The answer is, "He did!" John 3:16 says that He loved the world so much that He gave His only Son, so that whoever would believe in Him would not perish in hell but would have eternal life in heaven. The gospel message could not be clearer than that. Then He sent you and me—the Christians of the world—to take this good news to the ends of the earth. We are God's answer to the world's needs. That is why God sends out missionaries, for if people would know and serve God, most other matters would be settled.

At first, this may seem simplistic and maybe even fanatical; however, the truth is that until people's hearts are converted the outer effects of an inner condition will not change. As the father said to his daughter, "It's not the world, it's us."

Two Kinds of Missionaries

By now you may be convinced that the subject of world missions is so important that every church ought to have a systematic plan of missions education for its congregation. However, before we can develop such a plan, we must have a clear definition of what we mean by the word *missionary.*

We use the word for such a wide range of ministries and work locations that the word may have lost some of its original meaning. One dictionary defines the word *missionary* as "a person sent on a mission; specifically, a person sent out by his church to preach, teach, and proselyte in a foreign country, especially in one considered heathen." This definition tells us what missionaries are, where they are to go, and what they are to do when they get there.

If this definition is true, why do we refer to some who minister in our own country as home missionaries? The reason is that our own land is as heathen as any place on earth. Therefore, the church must not stop at sending missionaries to foreign lands, but must also appoint national missionaries to start and maintain new churches and to minister to special-need groups that might otherwise be neglected by the usual ministries of local churches. We must send missionaries wherever there are heathen (non-Christian) people in need of a Savior, at home or abroad.

Christians believe that Jesus Christ is the only way to God (John 14:6). All other religions, no matter how time-honored, respected, or followed, fail to pass the ultimate test of a genuine relationship with the real God. All other religions are man seeking God, but Christianity is God seeking man!

Foreign Missionaries

Let's try our own definition for *missionaries:* "Foreign missionaries are ministers who respond to God's call and are sent out by the church for evangelistic service outside their own country."

Strictly speaking, no two missionaries are alike. Every mission field is different, and the ministries of different missionaries in the same locality may be quite different. The Great Commission calls for the evangelization of every person in every community in every country. This requires many kinds of ministries in a great variety of living conditions. Many missionaries work basically at direct or mass evangelism, while others are in pastoral and church care, schools or orphanages, children's and youth ministries, military ministries, teaching, administration, or the translation, writing, printing, or distribution of literature. And, no matter what his or her other activities, a missionary will almost always teach in a Bible school for the preparation of national ministers.

The world is a complicated place, so missionary work is extremely diversified and constantly changing. Alfred Lord Tennyson wrote, "The old order changeth, yielding place to new."[1] The world has been changing so rapidly in the last few years that mapmakers cannot keep up with the shifting and renaming of countries, and writers cannot prepare textbooks fast enough to be current on social, political, and cultural changes.

The world is a moving target! Taking the gospel effectively to this ever-changing planet and making Christian converts is like trying to follow a car on the Los Angeles Freeway during rush hour. It is in this kaleidoscopic, ever-shifting, uncertain, and sinful world that missionaries must live and work. They must be some of the most adaptable and dedicated people the church has to offer for the service of our Lord.

Home Missionaries

Let's try another definition of *missionaries:* "Home missionaries are ministers who respond to God's call and are sent out by the church for evangelistic service inside their own country."

The key to understanding the word *missionary* is to realize that it refers to people who are sent out by the church to preach the gospel, teach, make converts, and establish churches among heathen or unchurched people. Being a foreign or a home missionary is of equal importance because God calls each minister to seek and to do His will. We sing an old missionary song, "I'll Go Where You Want Me To Go," with words written by Mary Brown and Charles E. Prior:

> I'll go where you want me to go, dear Lord,

O'er mountain, or plain, or sea;
I'll say what you want me to say, dear Lord,
I'll be what you want me to be.[2]

A personal commitment to the call and will of God is foundational to all Christian ministries, whether the mountains we cross are the Andes, the Alps, the Atlas Chain, or the Appalachians. The only real difference between home and foreign missionaries is the arena in which these Spirit warriors launch their challenge of light against the darkness.

A Separate Organization

Once we have admitted the geographical differences between home and foreign missions, we face the obvious conclusion that the selection, preparation, and administration of foreign missionaries is so different from that of home missionaries that the two kinds of missionary work must be organized separately. In the Assemblies of God, foreign-missions work is carried out through the Division of Foreign Missions, led by its executive director and a worldwide network of supervisors. Home-missions work is coordinated through the Division of Home Missions, led by its executive director and various departmental administrators.

The home-missions program does not require a large network of supervisors because all of its work happens within the American districts. For example, home missionaries of many districts minister among the Native American population of Arizona. They are *national* home missionaries and yet are responsible to coordinate their ministry with the Arizona District. Meanwhile, the Arizona District appoints its own home missionaries to plant new churches or to care for churches under district supervision. Still other national home missionaries may work among college students, gang members, the deaf, the blind, the military, or ethnic minorities, such as Iranians or Cambodians. Such is the work of the American home missionary.

We must think of home missions as essentially made up of

two kinds of ministry: (1) specialized ministries to minority groups, college campuses, the military, and people with specific needs, such as the blind or the deaf, or those with life-controlling problems; and (2) the ministries of starting new churches, or pastoring small and developing works. Most of the first group are coordinated by the Division of Home Missions, while most church planting and small-church care is carried out by the districts. For example, in the Northern California–Nevada District the assistant district superintendent and the World Missions Board he chairs supervise the work of 190 home-missions churches out of a total of 420 churches in the district. We must not see the diversification of home missions as a weakness, for its very strength is its ability to respond to the call of God to meet any new challenge with a minimum of organizational superstructure.

Beyond the Comfort Zone

Missionary work anywhere in the world, at home or abroad, involves great sacrifices; however, no sacrifice seems too great when we know that God has called us. The Assemblies of God has been blessed by many highly motivated ministers who have left their comfort zone of pastoring American sovereign churches to devote their lives to reaching the lost in more arduous areas. The inner-city pastor living in the dangerous, decaying ghetto, the foreign missionaries living in a remote West African town while their children are a thousand miles away in a boarding school, the home missionary dedicating himself to ministry to the deaf, the foreign missionary family continuing to work for God in the midst of a revolution—these are truly the heroes of our times!

Glamour, Grind, and Gratitude

Sometimes an unnecessary tension exists between home and foreign missions, due to inaccurate perceptions, the different natures of the work, and matters of fund-raising. A glamour of high adventure is associated with foreign service, especially in exotic lands, while in America we may think of home missions in terms of small churches and special-interest groups. Besides, home missionaries are working right at our own doorstep, so we can see their struggles, heartaches, and discouragements. Their successes may not seem dramatic because the numbers are often small. Pastors and congregations in established churches seldom remember the sense of victory in having 25 people come to the church at the same time.

Foreign missionaries have the advantages of distance and time. Few people ever see their work, and they usually have 4 years before they come home to report to the churches. Foreign missionaries may have trouble with a new language, fail to adjust to an alien culture, and spend most of their time writing letters and going after the mail—and still come home to a hero's welcome. Just the fact that they went out to the heathen world at all and plan to go back is often perceived as proof of their calling. But home missionaries receive little thanks for their labors and have few benchmarks by which their work may be judged. Home-missions pastors who do a good job sometimes move on to self-supporting churches and cease to be home missionaries. Those who remain with home-missions ministry as a career often struggle financially or have to work at other jobs to support their families. All of these factors lead to a rather vague image of what a home missionary is.

Two things are required to give home missionaries the right image and the honor due them: (1) better fund-raising to get the financial support needed for their work, and (2) better communication with supporting churches.

Before foreign missionaries take pen in hand to write in response to the last two paragraphs, let us quickly agree that there are few hero's welcomes, brass bands, "Welcome Home" banners, or cheering crowds when missionaries return to America, although some thoughtful churches do provide wonderful exceptions to the rule. When a foreign missionary comes home after 4 years of blood, sweat, and tears, usually a supporting pastor asks, "Oh, are you home already? When are you going back?"

Before all the pastors reading this object, let us agree that what the supporting pastor means is, "I know you will want to come and thank our people for their financial and prayer support. How much time do we have to work you into our church schedule before you return to your field?"

Of course, the missionary then wonders how much he or she is loved if the churches are not just jumping at the opportunity to meet the missionary and hear his or her story.

Both foreign and home missionaries may have trouble coping with few outward expressions of gratitude and appreciation. But it doesn't stop there! All of us—pastors, Sunday school teachers, missions committees, district officials and members of district boards, executives and staff members of the national Divisions of Foreign and Home Missions—yes, and maybe even the general superintendent—may share the same experience; namely, that other people seldom understand what we do or know how to thank us. We realize that when we give our heart to God for His service we no longer live for praise or promotion. Jesus said, "As my Father hath sent me, even so send I you" (John 20:21). Jesus was misunderstood, mistreated, and martyred, yet He lived only for His Father's approval. "This is my beloved Son, in whom I am well pleased" (Matthew 3:17). We all need approval and appreciation, but in the work of the Lord we have to decide for whom we are working, what we are to do, and where we are to do it. Then we will labor joyfully and wholeheartedly with or without human thanks.

But there is more. Throughout the whole system—between fellow missionaries, between missionaries and their sending boards, and between missionaries and supporting pastors and churches—there should be mutual respect and appreciation. Both home and foreign missions require high levels of personal commitment and courage. Each missionary has his or her special place in our hearts and in God's heart.

Because of the great variety of ministries and methods involved in home missions, this book cannot cover all the aspects of how to become a home missionary. In the following section we will look at how a person becomes a foreign missionary. Many of the same factors apply to becoming a home missionary.

How To Become a Foreign Missionary

Most missionaries sense their divine calling early in life. Some have a spiritual experience in prayer or in a dream in which they sense the Lord's voice and receive their *call.* Others have a moment of realization, perhaps in a church service or missions convention, when they discover their calling. However, most missionaries do not trace their missionary call to a single event or experience but testify to a growing sense of need and burden for lost humanity. This process generally begins in their childhood, grows through their youth, and matures in their young adult life. Most missionary candidates say their interest in missions began in their early Sunday school years.

Responding to the Call

No one kind of missionary calling seems to be superior to the others. How a person is called is not as important as how he or she responds. In addition to the challenges of the missionaries' work as soul winners, church planters, Bible school teachers, and much more, missionaries face the difficulties of learning a foreign language, adapting to other cultures, often living and working in life-threatening circumstances, and coping with wars, famines, and terrible human need. Because of all these challenges foreign missionaries must be among the most dedicated Christians in the world, and among the most committed people to a cause.

Except for a few special ministries, the route for becoming a missionary is to graduate from a Bible college and become a full-time minister. Some people enter their missionary career after having served as an assistant pastor or in some other church staff position, but their foreign ministry generally will be strongest if they have pastored a church on their own. Much of a missionary's work is in training and helping pastors of small churches, so the missionary without pastoral experience may be seriously handicapped. The opening of new fields requires highly skilled people, and the work of developed fields calls for missionaries with more experience than that of the national pastors with whom they work. In either case, the missionary needs both a solid Bible college education and a wealth of pastoral experience, and yet must still be young enough to learn a new language and adapt to a new culture.

People who believe they qualify for foreign missionary service because of their calling, education, health, ministerial experience, and other qualities may write to the Assemblies of God Division of Foreign Missions (1445 Boonville Avenue, Springfield, Missouri 65802–1894) or to other denominational offices or missions boards to ask about their application procedure. Naturally, all mission societies are looking for candidates who have already proven their calling by winning people to Christ and producing a growing church in their own homeland. After all, how can we expect anyone to win a nation to Christ in another culture who cannot minister successfully in his or her own culture?

Quality Training and Experience

Foreign-missions leaders are often torn between two equally important and yet mutually exclusive needs in the selection and training of missionary candidates. On the one hand, missionaries desperately need quality education followed by 2 or more years of pastoral experience. They should be ordained ministers with at least a 4-year degree. That is basic, because a college degree may be required to obtain a visa to live in a country and because the ministry of most missionaries includes working with pastors and teaching in a Bible school. By the time a candidate qualifies, he or she will probably be 26 to 30 years of age, married, and have children. The raising of children and the maintenance of normal family life are among the most serious problems on the mission field. On the other hand, the need for education and ministerial experience must be balanced with that of language learning and intercultural adaptation. Generally, the older we get the harder it is to learn a new language or to cope with the confusion of a different culture. The consequences of the Tower of Babel are still with us, and some of our most serious international misunderstandings stem from ethnolinguistic differences—a fancy term for how people think and talk.

Short-Term Missions Experience

The Assemblies of God encourages high school and college students (16 to 28 years old) to participate in short-term missionary ministry with AIM (Ambassadors in Mission). College-age and older people may serve in either the home or foreign missions MAPS programs, or in an internship program called MIT (Missionaries in Training). Still, the most highly recommended route to the mission field is through Bible college graduation, ordination with the Assemblies of God, and experience in pastoring.

Budget and Itinerating

After being recommended by his or her district, processed by the Division of Foreign Missions, and approved by the Foreign Missions Board, a missionary candidate must travel among the churches to present the missionary challenge and to seek financial and prayer support. Each missionary is given a budget to raise—an amount of money needed for fare, freight, equipment, and other initial costs and an amount required in monthly support pledges. These monthly pledges often continue throughout the missionary's career but certainly must extend through the first foreign term, usually 4 years.

People sometimes are surprised by the funds most missionaries have to raise, but the amounts they require for reaching a nation are really quite modest compared to the monthly budgets of most local churches in America. Let us say, for example, that a missionary has to raise $5,000 per month to support his family and carry out his work. That would be only $60,000 a year, considerably less than the annual budget of most self-supporting churches in America. If we are having trouble reaching our neighborhoods with that kind of money, how do we expect a missionary to win a nation? We need to get serious about the Great Commission and have every church increase its commitments to home- and foreign-missionary support.

We often use the word *itineration* to describe what missionaries do during their 12 to 18 months of raising their support. They itinerate or travel among the churches. The term *deputation* is also used for the same activity. This method of supporting missionaries has two advantages:

1. The missionary gathers a group of supporting churches and individuals who will pray and sponsor him or her financially.

2. The missionary's travel among the churches prepares the former local minister for a broader scale of ministry. Most foreign-missionary work is more like the ministry of a district superintendent than like that of a pastor.

Choosing a Field

The two basic varieties of church government are congregational and episcopal. Congregational churches are owned and operated by their congregations, which write their own bylaws and elect their own pastors. The Assemblies of God is a good example of congregational church government. However, when a minister becomes a missionary, he or she becomes part of an episcopal form of government in which properties are held in the denomination's name and ministers are *appointed.* For example, in the Northern California–Nevada District all home-missions properties are held by the district, and the home-missions pastors are appointed by the World Missions Board. Much the same thing happens for foreign missionaries, who are appointed by the Foreign Missions Board.

In actual practice, the choice of a mission field is a cooperative process that considers the individual's sense of calling, the needs on the field, and the current opportunities for service. If a missionary candidate says, "I feel called to Paraguay," every effort will be made to get him or her there. However, if there is a crying need for a missionary in nearby Uruguay, the missionary might be asked to pray about an alternate opportunity. Many missionary candidates name only a preferred continent or ask to go to the place of greatest need. Also, many missionaries do not feel so much called to a place as to a kind of ministry. Some respond best to undeveloped fields, while others are more adapted to the structure of established ministries. We have come to trust the process by which the wishes of the individual, the counsel of the brethren, and the will of God come together by prayer to determine a missionary's correct choice of a foreign field.

The whole missionary operation is based on the strategic appointments of devoted men and women in cooperation with missionaries, pastors, churches, district offices, national administrators, and the ever-changing opportunities offered by God in a world turned sideways.

---

[1]*The Oxford Dictionary of Quotations.* (New York: Oxford University Press, 1979), 535.

[2]Mary Brown and Charles E. Prior, "I'll Go Where You Want Me To Go" in *Hymns of Glorious Praise* (Springfield, Mo.: Gospel Publishing House, 1969), 277.

5
Getting It All Together

Four blind men inspected an elephant. One of them found the animal's leg and declared, "An elephant is like a tree." Another found the tail and announced, "An elephant is like a rope." Yet another found the trunk and said, "An elephant is like a vine." And the fourth man found the leathery side and claimed, "An elephant is like a wall."

A Limited Vision

All of us are limited in our vision and incomplete in our knowledge. The old story above continues to live because it points out the important observation that we tend to see things in part rather than as a whole. Sometimes we say of a person who lacks a broad view of things that he can't see the forest for the trees.

When it comes to missions education in the local church, we are particularly apt to work with partial information and a limited understanding because the world is too big for any one person to comprehend. We each bring a different viewpoint based on fragmentary knowledge and limited experience.

For example, the people in a church might hear a missionary speak, see children participating in Boys and Girls Missionary Crusade, observe the Women's Ministries ladies sending birthday gifts and cards to missionaries, attend a Light–for–the–Lost banquet sponsored by Men's Ministries, see young people washing cars for Speed–the–Light, read in the church bulletin about a group of teenagers going to Mexico for an Ambassadors in Mission trip, meet a retired couple going to Egypt to help missionaries under the Missions Abroad Placement Service, or hear the testimony of a layman who has just returned from an inner-city church-building project with the Mission America Placement Service, without realizing that these programs are all part of one integrated system for world evangelism.

The Assemblies of God foreign- and home-missions programs are well-designed to send out missionaries and support them with all they require to do their work and fulfill the Great Commission. What we need today is for every local church to integrate its missions emphasis to take full advantage of the whole system and to involve every person in the congregation in world missions.

The Growing Other Half

Do you remember those first pictures the astronauts took of the earth? They showed us a beautiful planet, but half the world was in darkness!

Half the world is still in darkness, because about 3 billion of the nearly 6 billion people now living on earth have not yet heard enough of the gospel to know how to accept Jesus Christ as Savior and Lord. No matter how successful our missions program, the task of world evangelization is not yet half done. A few years ago, the Assemblies of God rejoiced that it had reached a constituency of 50,000 believers in India. The celebration was dampened when we discovered that the population of India was then growing by 50,000 people a day! Our whole church in India was equal to one day's population growth.

We face a huge task of educating people to a greater and more intense level of missionary endeavor. Missions education must permeate the church from nursery classes to senior ministries and from local churches to "the uttermost part of the earth" (Acts 1:8). This new wave of missions education must both prepare a new generation of missionaries and supporters, and reorient the missionaries themselves, because what we are doing now will not evangelize the world in our time.

In Pentecostal churches, we absorb much of our attitude about missions from the general evangelistic state of mind of our Movement. Pentecostal people believe that Jesus is coming back again and that only those who believe in Him are saved. Combine that sense of evangelistic urgency with the intensity that comes from the Baptism, and you will understand what has driven our missionaries to the ends of the earth.

The phenomenal growth of the Pentecostal movement in the 20th century did not result from any carefully orchestrated missions strategy but from the nature of the Movement itself. Highly inspired and committed missionaries went out with little preparation or language training, little financial support, and limited knowledge of the cultures they were seeking to change. The miracle was that it worked! The national people who converted to Christ were also filled with the Holy Spirit, and they began to carry the gospel to their own people with the same fervor that had driven the missionaries.

Why, then, do we need missions education today? It would be easy to weep for the loss of a simpler and perhaps more purely Pentecostal time, but we would be wrong. We have more dedicated, Spirit-filled missionaries today, winning more souls to Christ, and resulting in more lasting successes than at any time in our history. The truth is we have learned many things about missions, and we must pass our knowledge down to the next generation. In the early years, our missionaries were dealing with a less complicated time when people of many areas were open to new ideas from the more developed countries. But in today's difficult, often dangerous world both the missionaries and those who send them must be more knowledgeable and more skilled at language and intercultural communication.

Educational Skills

The very phrase "missions education in the local church" infers that we must possess some educational skills to carry out our purpose. Few pastors have received such training, and even fewer of the people involved in teaching in their churches have had any formal training. The leaders in the national Sunday School Promotion and Training Department are well-trained in the philosophies and methods of modern education and provide valuable help through their printed materials and ministry in the districts. Only larger churches can afford to have ministers of Christian education. Smaller churches sometimes are blessed by having schoolteachers in their congregations, but they often must do the best they can with few resources.

Believe it or not, the idea of Sunday school is older than the modern concept of public education in America. Robert Raikes established the first modern Sunday school in Gloucester, England, in 1780.[1] In those more difficult times, many children worked in factories every day but Sunday, so he began to hold Sunday classes in the homes of lay teachers. The idea spread throughout England and Wales and was introduced to the United States in 1791.

Today's public school system came mostly out of the 19th century, although every culture in every age has had some way of teaching culture, history, and skills to its young. The idea of offering the same education to all children is relatively new and still questioned by some.

Preschool Level

Preschool educational programs are based on the concept of learning through play. Through guided play, children learn about themselves and the world around them, organize what they know into conceptual patterns, and learn to express themselves to share what they know. Some of the most effective preschool programs use classroom centers with different activities or playthings. Rather than trying to get all the preschoolers to do the same thing together at the same time, they seek to capture the child's curiosity and interest. Play in these areas is often alternated with more structured activities, such as listening to stories, being involved in discussions, watching films or videos, and joining in cleanup and self-care. Including parents from time to time in the preschool learning process is also very effective.

In such a setting, church teachers have excellent opportunities to introduce preschool children to world missions by providing foreign dolls or other objects among their American toys, by showing pictures of foreign children and animals, and by telling missionary and Bible stories.

Let us not forget that the study of the Bible itself is an exercise in intercultural learning. All the Bible stories happened in other times, in other cultures, and in other languages. The Bible is one of the best tools of missions education in the local church.

Elementary Level

Elementary education has been in some disarray in recent years. Early schools relied heavily on rote learning, but today's schools tend to concentrate on skill acquisition and cognitive development. They emphasize the development of the whole child, stressing social and emotional adjustment, resolving social inequalities, training the child in serving the needs of society, and equipping the child for economic and social progress. In other words, much of today's primary education is aimed at a sociological restructuring of society rather than at developing children to work within their society. The 1980 census showed that 96 percent of American children between the ages of 5 and 13 were enrolled in kindergarten through 8th grade.[2]

With the amount of social experimentation going on and the problems of drugs and low moral standards in the public schools, more parents are opting for private schools, many of which are operated by churches or church-oriented groups. Other parents feel they would rather teach their children to cope with the world by guiding them through Christian homes and churches. It is a difficult problem for today's parents.

Secondary Level

High schools were slower in developing than grade schools.

In 1910 only 15 percent of the children aged 14 through 17 were enrolled in high school, 32 percent in 1920, just over 50 percent in 1930, 73 percent in 1940, 77 percent in 1950, 87 percent in 1960, and 94 percent in 1970. The National Education Association's Commission on the Reorganization of Secondary Education recommends seven cardinal principles as objectives of today's high schools: (1) health, (2) command of fundamental processes (reading, writing, speaking, and arithmetic), (3) worthy home-membership, (4) vocation, (5) citizenship, (6) worthy use of leisure, and (7) ethical character.[3]

A church's Sunday school must be geared to complement the work of primary and secondary schools. Bible learning and the application of its truths are at the heart of the curriculum. Missions education occurs within the whole context of Christian education.

A New Orientation for Missionaries

Early Pentecostals had to learn a lesson about inspiration, or what we call the "anointing." Many of them did not put much faith in sermon preparation out of fear that their study might hinder the flow of the Spirit. They used to quote Psalm 81:10: "I am the Lord thy God . . . open thy mouth wide, and I will fill it."

The anointed preacher was seen as a sort of human funnel through which the Holy Spirit would pour His message without the preacher's adding to or subtracting from the flow. However, over the years we have discovered that we are not so much like funnels as we are like storehouses of experience and learning. The Holy Spirit brings forth the flow of motivated preaching from our personal storehouses and adds His own elements of inspiration and sensitivity. The more knowledge, wisdom, and skills we store the more effectively the Holy Spirit may use us for His purposes. Anointed preaching is a cooperative effort between the preacher and the Lord. Pentecostal Christians should be the most creative people in the world because they are filled with the Spirit of the Creator.

THE INDIGENOUS CHURCH

Over the years missionaries have worked under a great anointing, both in preaching and in discovering creative solutions to world evangelism. One of the most inspired concepts is called the *indigenous church*—the idea that the church of Jesus Christ will grow naturally within any culture in which it is introduced. That is, we don't go into a country to set up an American church; we set up a national church with workers, pastors, and, eventually, national leaders coming out of the people being converted. The idea received its first practical application and development in Central America, especially by Missionary Ralph Williams. Missionary Melvin L. Hodges worked with Williams and later became the field secretary for Latin America and the Caribbean. His book *The Indigenous Church* became the definitive work on the subject.[4] This concept has opened the world to the Assemblies of God and has gained great respect from national believers and the whole world-missions community.

Although indigenous-church thinking has largely benefited world missions and has developed a large number of national ministers, it has within it four long-term problems:

1. Missionaries tend to relinquish vital leadership before national Christians are prepared to receive such responsibilities.
2. The goal tends to become that of establishing a national church organization rather than evangelizing the whole country.
3. Missionaries tend to back off from front-line evangelism and busy themselves with administration, program development, and institutions.
4. The strong emphasis on the superiority of the national church makes it too nationalistic.

The indigenous-church concept is itself somewhat paternalistic because it assumes we go into a country to teach the national pastors how to organize their church and reach their own country. If the earlier father-to-child approach of missions was paternalistic, the indigenous approach of teacher to adolescent is often pedagogic. What needs to follow the indigenous-church stage is a new and more grown-up internationalism in which the Lord may place His servants by their calling and skills rather than by the limited definitions of national boundaries. We are in need of a new revival of preaching, teaching, and convert-making—the basic elements of the Great Commission.

Educational Level of Missionaries

The Division of Foreign Missions has made great strides in raising the educational level of its missionaries and training them in its philosophies and techniques. Over the years, the program has enjoyed the great advantage of having so many qualified, Spirit-filled people available for foreign service that it has been able to be selective. However, when ministers become missiologists rather than missionaries they run the terrible risk of viewing the human race from the outside, rather than plunging heart-deep into the realities of identification with people, their cultures, and their languages.

This more intellectual and more managerial approach to missions is working only because the world has been moving toward increased westernization. Many people overseas like the American style and seek to emulate it, so missionaries are able to carry out their ministries in a typically American way. Yet, the finest missionaries always have been the career people who leave family and homeland behind and immerse themselves in their divine task within the context of another country, language, and culture.

One of today's buzz phrases is *transcultural communication,* a term that helps missionaries describe the problem of relating to people who are different from themselves. The very idea that missionaries must communicate across cultural gaps between themselves and the people they seek to influence is an admission of alienation. Jesus did not come to communicate with us across the chasm between heaven and earth, but to identify with us in the Incarnation, by which He became one of us and spoke to us from within our world and in the context of our culture. We must take seriously the words of our Lord, "As my Father hath sent me, even so send I you" (John 20:21).

The Unfinished Task

In our enthusiasm over our successes, it is easy to overestimate our effectiveness and to take lightly the appalling dimensions of the unfinished task. We may easily become victims of our own promotional strategies. One foreign-missions leader in his personal news release speaks of "a united thrust of fraternal Assemblies of God fellowships to achieve worldwide evangelization by the year 2000." Public relations notwithstanding, in the absence of a worldwide revival, what we are doing today is not going to evangelize the world in our times. Jesus may return any day and our task will be completed; however, we must continue planning to reach the lost beyond the year 2000. Only the Father knows the day of Christ's return.

The Real Need

We should continue to expand our current efforts to reach the world. We must have Bible schools, construction projects, home-study courses, special ministries to youth and to the military, and literature production and distribution—the whole business of missions. But we need a revival of old-fashioned, down-to-earth, individualistic, and probably fanatical missionaries who will inspire a fervent Christian movement that will take the flame from our controlled bonfires and set fire to the whole woods!

Police departments in many communities have noted the growing resentment of citizens for any action by the police, even if it is in the people's defense. Police officers are usually not known personally because they always drive around in cars and get out only when somebody is in trouble. Returning some police officers to walking beats in the communities enables them to get acquainted with the people. It has greatly improved their public image and their effectiveness in preventing and dealing with crime. A similar need has developed on most mission fields as gaps continue to grow between missionaries and the very people God has called them to evangelize and develop. We have to get the gospel back into the streets and marketplaces of the world.

No matter how many programs we set up or how many contemporary technologies we employ, we are not going to evangelize the world from offices and committee meetings. We need real people on the ground with Bibles in their hands, the Spirit of God in their hearts, and fire in their eyes. Of course, we cannot run this vast worldwide operation without management specialists and team missionaries. However, we also cannot evangelize the world without those determined individuals who plunge into personal identification with another culture, come into spiritual conflict with evil in that society, and then rise to greatness for God within that setting. This often happens at the expense of the understanding of the American church or their missionary peers. Only out of such a fire ignited deeply within the heart of another culture can we ever hope to evangelize the world.

A Missions Paradigm

To create this kind of missionary, we must change our thinking about missions in the local church. In that way, our appointments of leaders from local missions coordinators to district world-missions directors to national positions of influence and administration will insist on a renewed emphasis on high-priority, high-motivation, high-intensity evangelism. Missionaries for such a revival must come from the local churches that are carrying out the same kind of evangelism in their own communities. We need candidates who grow up in churches where they hear about missions, observe souls being saved, participate in evangelism in their childhood and youth, and develop in a deeply spiritual environment of salvation, healing, and deliverance. Give us churches like that and we will provide an army of fiery-eyed missionaries with some chance at total world evangelization.

Integrating the Local Missions Program

We must decide if we, as a local church, are truly committed to total world evangelization or if we are satisfied with only a token presence in each country. Is it enough to say we have established a national church, or must we continue on to evangelize the whole country? A few local churches are very organized in their world-missions outreach, but most need to unite their fragmentary missions involvements into a single integrated ministry.

We must realize that not all church programs are the same. Even though for practical purposes a church may have a Sunday school department, Sunday school itself is not a department in the same sense as departments for youth, music, or women's and men's auxiliaries because Sunday school is the whole church studying God's Word. Similarly, the church's world-missions program is the whole church in its ministries to the whole world. "The Whole Church for the Whole World!"—wouldn't that be a good theme for a missions convention?

Purpose and Plan

What do we actually mean by an integrated world-missions program in the local church?

1. All we do for world missions is tied together by a single purpose.
2. All the different missions-oriented programs are built together into a single plan.

Before we can do anything in this regard, we must define what we are doing and why we are doing it. Try the following statement of purpose (built on biblical principles) for a local church:

> The purpose of this church's world-missions program is to carry out the Great Commission of Jesus Christ in the world by training, motivating, and involving the congregation in community, national, and world evangelism and by preparing, sending, and supporting foreign and home missionaries.

By this local-church statement of purpose, we may identify ourselves with the original commands of Jesus; commit ourselves to the three missions-education elements of training, motivation, and involvement; and work toward the preparation, sending, and support of missionaries.

A Trained and Prepared Congregation

To carry out such a purpose, what would the average church have to change? We have done fairly well with *motivation* and *involvement* and with *sending* and *supporting* missionaries, primarily because of the intensity of the Pentecostal movement and the itineration of missionaries. To encourage our churches to grow and to reach a broader range of Americans, we must strengthen our local missions programs by increasing the *training* and *preparation* of each congregation. All our people need training to understand and support missions, and those who will be in full-time ministries need preparation from the earliest years in the nursery until they leave us for further education and experience.

We need to look at the whole process rather than seeing our missions elements as separate or unrelated programs. What Sunday school children do when they put pennies in a BGMC Buddy Barrel bank is related to what young people do for Speed–the–Light or what adults do through faith promises. Every church ministry must have some kind of world-missions orientation, and all the different ministries must be related to each other. We need pastors who will see the church's missions ministries as a whole. If the pastor understands the missions concept then he can train others. Many pastors appoint a world-missions coordinator to represent the church's missions ministry and to relate with the departmental and auxiliary ministries. Any church of any size can do that. Larger churches will have a committee or department to coordinate the ministries, generate financial and prayer support, and plan the church's annual or semiannual missions convention.

A church's missionary identity grows out of its outlook and understanding of its place in God's plan. That vision leads to specific programs intended to involve people in missions and to help the missionaries. In Assemblies of God churches missionary training is done with all ages and groups in the congregation.

Start With Children

Missions education begins with the youngest children, who need to grow up in an environment where they may see missionaries often and hear their pastor, parents, and teachers speak favorably about missions. They need to have ample opportunity to be saved, filled with the Holy Spirit, and called by God. As children are involved with Sunday school and children's church, they are introduced to Boys and Girls Missionary Crusade (BGMC), a program that teaches children about missions and trains them to respond by praying and giving money to provide missionaries with Christian education and evangelism resources. Children also receive missions education through Missionettes and Royal Rangers, scouting-type programs that often include missions and missionary projects.

Continue With Teens

When children enter their teenage years, they become involved in giving and raising money for Speed–the–Light (STL), a youth ministry that provides transportation and communication equipment for evangelism. As a result of STL, missionaries have smaller budgets to raise because STL provides a vehicle for every missionary. Teens also join FIRE prayer groups to pray for world evangelism. The national Youth Department's Ambassadors in Mission (AIM) sponsors short-term evangelistic campaigns overseas and in the United States for high school and college youth. Many young people have felt called to missionary service after spending a week or two on a mission field.

Provide Opportunities for Adults

Young ministers may benefit from the program Missionaries in Training, which allows them to go overseas before qualifying for full missionary service.

People who possess needed skills in construction, secretarial work, education, or other professions may go to a mission field to assist the missionaries under a program called Missions Abroad and Placement Service (MAPS). Often retired persons give some years of overseas service through MAPS. The Division of Home Missions calls its MAPS program the Mission America Placement Service.

Many adults get involved with missions through Women's or Men's Ministries. The women of our churches work constantly to outfit the missionaries' homes and wardrobes and to raise money for missionary projects. The men of our Fellowship raise money for evangelistic literature through Light–for–the–Lost. Some districts hold banquets or "steak-outs," where they receive pledges from local men's groups.

Most young people and adults also get involved with world evangelism through their local church's programs, such as the annual world-missions convention or the faith-promise plan (see chapter 6). Some churches never give to missions or have missionary speakers in their pulpits, but the majority see missionaries often and give to missions regularly.

Follow the Fundamentals

A successful local missions program has three fundamental parts.

1. *Have missionary speakers often.* Many churches have a missionary guest at least once every 2 months, and many have more missionary services than that. Most churches that give

$10,000 or more annually to foreign and home missions have 12 or more missionary speakers each year.

2. *Use the faith-promise plan to raise monthly missionary funds in the congregation.* The system works so smoothly and so well that many successful churches never need to take up a special missions offering unless a missionary is present who needs a cash offering.

3. *Hold an annual world-missions convention.* All successful missions-minded churches hold some kind of annual special missions emphasis. Some do it twice a year and ask their people for 6-month commitments.

Some churches involve their people in missions by mothering new churches, by sending out teams for construction and other projects for home-missions churches, or by sending teams overseas to build churches or Bible schools or to assist in evangelistic efforts.

Proper missions education in the local church requires that the pastor and others in leadership see the various missions elements as part of an integrated whole rather than as separate, unrelated programs. BGMC leads to Speed–the–Light, which leads to the range of adult responses to missions. If we are really serious about the Great Commission and the soon coming of Jesus Christ, we must raise our standards and improve our effectiveness.

Remember, more than half the world is still in darkness!

---

[1]Stephen Rexroat, *The Sunday School Spirit* (Springfield, Mo.: Gospel Publishing House, 1979), 12.

[2]*Academic American Encyclopedia.* (Danbury, Conn.: Grolier Electronic Publishing, 1992), "Primary Education," by Erwin V. Johanningmeier, 16 (Prodigy).

[3]*Academic American Encyclopedia.* (Danbury, Conn.: Grolier Electronic Publishing, 1992), "Secondary Education," by Erwin V. Johanningmeier, 15 (Prodigy).

[4]Melvin L. Hodges, *The Indigenous Church* (Springfield, Mo.: Gospel Publishing House, 1976), order number 02–0527.

6
A World-Missions Celebration

On a Sunday morning in a church in north Texas, the congregation became silent in expectation of the "World Missions Parade" promised in the church bulletin. A drum roll sounded, and the missions coordinator announced, "Ladies and Gentlemen, representing tribes and nations from the uttermost parts of the earth, we present this year's World Missions Parade!"

Music began, and the crowd broke into chuckles as preschool children and first- and second-graders marched into the sanctuary dressed in foreign costumes and carrying placards identifying their countries. One blue-eyed blond girl in a Japanese kimono walked down the aisle with tiny steps, pausing to bow politely to the crowd. An African-American girl carrying a bouquet of tulips was attired in a Dutch outfit complete with wooden shoes. And a 4-year-old Hispanic boy wore dark glasses and a flowing white Arabian burnoose and carried a gasoline can.

The rest of the children of the Sunday school followed in creative costumes from many lands. Behind them came the youth group with the girls wearing pretty foreign dresses and the boys outfitted in military camouflage and other revolutionary uniforms. They all sat in the front pews while a missionary speaker brought a message on winning the world for Christ. Afterward the children and youth went to their departmental booths, where they served snacks that could have come from their chosen lands.

Did those costumes or booths really contribute much to world missions? Absolutely yes! The children and youth were all keyed up for that service and they sat in the front rows ready to be influenced for God. The parents and the Sunday school teachers were involved in making the costumes and booths, and the church increased both its missions awareness and giving.

One critic of missions conventions once said, "You reduce world missions to a sort of county fair!" Well, that's the point! A county fair is where the local farmers bring their prize animals and produce to celebrate what they have accomplished out in the fields. People come from far and wide to see their successes and become motivated to go back home and grow or make something of prize-winning quality for the next year. A county fair is a celebration of the county's productivity and growth. And that's also what a missions convention is for the local church.

To have a strong world-missions program, a local church must plan an annual missions emphasis to celebrate what has been done, to raise monthly faith-promises, and to look forward to future victories.

Communicate!

One of the most important elements of a successful world-missions program is *feedback.* This descriptive word is relatively new to the English language and almost impossible to translate into other languages. It comes from the world of electronics. According to one dictionary, it means "the feeding back of part of the output to the input at the proper phase; used in radio to amplify or decrease the strength of a signal." That is, part of the electronic output is brought back and fed into the system at the right time to alter it in some way. In the case of radio, a feedback system can take a weak signal and amplify or strengthen it for its area of reception.

Once the new word got into our language, it began to be used in other ways. For example, after a politician makes a speech on national television he might want a new poll to give him feedback—in this case, a measured change in public opinion.

Feedback is the response that indicates the success or failure of whatever has been done.

Let us say, for example, that a church contributes $10,000 a year to world missions. That may not be much compared to the hundreds of thousands of dollars given by a few very large churches, but when you add up the giving of all the small- to medium-sized churches the total makes up a significant part of the annual giving.

Where does the money come from? A few millionaires may give some significant donations, but most of the giving year-in and year-out comes from the cooperation and vision of the whole congregation. The money comes from working people who tithe 10 percent to the local church and voluntarily add another $50 a month to reach the world for Christ, from widows who sacrificially give of their meager income, from young people who are taught to proclaim their faith by sending out missionaries, and from pastors who often lead the way in missions giving in their congregations. The money comes from children dropping coins in their BGMC banks, from teenagers running marathons for Speed–the–Light, from women raising funds by selling craft items and baked goods, and from men holding steak-outs for Light–for–the–Lost. When you look at it that way, $10,000 is a lot of money that must be earned through hard work and yet is joyfully given to reach the world for Christ.

Positive Feedback to Wonderful People

Doesn't it make sense, then, that there should be an annual missions emphasis to give positive feedback to all those wonderful people? They are not demanding, but they do want to know if their efforts are effective and if their money is being distributed and spent wisely.

People need feedback and affirmation. That is, they need more than reports and sales pitches; they need factual information and the affirmation that what they are doing is right and worth the effort they are putting into the operation. Life is hard today, and only the most significant causes can be worth the people's giving up their hard-earned cash. Then, once they have decided that what they are doing is meaningful and worth the effort, they need the opportunity to celebrate their victories and consider new strategies for the challenges. After the Children of Israel crossed the Red Sea, Moses' sister Miriam brought out her tambourine and the Israelites celebrated their miracle. An annual missions emphasis gives the church the opportunity to get feedback, affirm its resolve, and celebrate. This puts the whole church into a growth mode and sets the stage for even greater giving and growing in the year ahead.

Paul's Example

The key is communication. The apostle Paul thanked "all the saints in Christ Jesus . . . at Philippi, with the bishops and deacons" (Philippians 1:1) for having sent him a missionary offering. He rejoiced that their care for him had "flourished again," commended them that they had done well, and thanked them that they had communicated with his affliction (Philippians 4:10,14). Apparently, he really needed their communication (offering) and responded to it by giving them feedback in his letter. He said, "Ye sent once and again unto my necessity. Not because I desire a gift: but I desire fruit that may abound to your account" (verses 16,17). So the Christians of Philippi were sending money regularly to support Paul's missionary work.

We often quote the encouraging words of Philippians 4:19, "My God shall supply all your need according to his riches in glory by Christ Jesus." However, many Bible readers do not realize that wonderful promise is made only to people who regularly send financial support to missionaries! God blesses a missionary-minded church and the individuals who stand behind missionaries with their prayers and finances. Notice the personal association, "my God." God does not bless just those who give money. Rather, the giving comes out of a personal relationship with God. To know Him is to stand behind His cause in the world. It is He who will supply all we need.

Observe also that He will supply all our need "according to his riches in glory by Christ Jesus." He does not draw on our meager bank account but on His riches in heaven through all that Jesus Christ has purchased for us by His life, death, and resurrection. God's help to us is not limited by any human resources but is poured out abundantly and without reservation. To this marvelous offer of divine assistance we all murmur a grateful, "Amen!"

But wait! More can be learned about this verse. Every promise of God must be understood in the setting in which it was made, for we cannot take a verse out of context and expect God to honor it. We must look carefully at the setting or context of the text. "Con" means " with," so the *context* means what goes with the text. Paul had just thanked the Christians of Philippi for communicating with him, by which he meant that they had sent money to support his missionary ministry. He said that God would keep record of their faithfulness in missions giving, and it was on that basis that he said, "My God shall supply all your need according to his riches in glory by Christ Jesus." In that context the promise is made to people who faithfully support the Lord's missionaries.

Paul no doubt had told the Philippians about his need. They had responded and had sent their offerings to support his work, and Paul responded by giving them the feedback of his thanks and God's blessings.

Paul called missionary support "communicating." Today we think of communication as a two-way exchange. One dictionary defines *communication* as "the exchange of thoughts, messages, or information." So we communicate with missionaries through our faithful giving and prayer, and they communicate back through newsletters, through occasional articles in the *Pentecostal Evangel* and other denominational and district publications, and by returning to our churches every few years to thank supporters and seek new support.

Much church work has to do with motivating and involving people in attendance, worship, participation in ministries, membership, and much more. No business or social venture relies more on human response and responsibility than the church. We must understand and use the important concept of feedback and affirmation to know how people are receiving communication and to increase future participation.

A Timbouctou Example

Let us say that a new missionary comes to your church and tells you God has called his family to Timbouctou in the West African nation of Mali. He says that 90 percent of the 9 million Malians are Muslim and that less than 1 percent are Christians. The church gives him a missionary offering and makes a monthly pledge of $50 to his support. He hands out cards with his name and a picture of his young family, and then he is gone for 4 to 5 years.

It was a good missionary service, but what happens now? Sometime after arriving on the mission field, the missionary writes home. Supporting churches should receive a letter from each of their missionaries at least every 3 months informing the congregation and encouraging continued prayer and support. If the church does not hear from a missionary, the people will forget him or her. The missions committee will conclude that the missionary probably does not need their monthly pledge, so they will transfer their support to another missionary who will stay in contact. World missions is a cooperative effort, requiring teamwork between those who send and those who are sent.

Missionary Furlough

When missionaries return to America on what is popularly called their furlough, they itinerate among their supporting churches and seek new support from other churches. Actually, it's not a furlough but an important part of their ministry. Assemblies of God missionaries get an annual vacation, often outside the country of their labors. They are to spend some time in rest and recreation when they return to America and then go back to work like everybody else. Their year of itineration among the churches is absolutely essential to the whole program because it exposes congregations to missionaries and motivates children and young people to become the next generation of missionaries. A missionary reports to supporting churches, who then feel they have done the right thing in supporting that missionary and continue their teamwork for another term.

Sadly, some missionaries do not return to their supporting churches when they come home but dedicate their time to making only new contacts. The truth is that there probably is more potential for increased support from those who already know and appreciate them than from strangers.

Church Support Statistics

Of course, there is another side to this problem. We are assuming that churches have organized world-missions programs, but such churches are far in the minority. According to the Assemblies of God Division of Foreign Missions, in 1991 some 5,108 churches gave less than $1,000 to foreign missions. Included in that figure were 2,009 churches that gave nothing at all. Think about it. That means 17.3 percent of Assemblies of God churches—almost 1 out of every 6 churches—gave not 1 cent to reach the world for Jesus Christ!

The number of churches that gave less than $5,000 for the year was 8,287, or 72 percent of the churches. Of every 100 churches, 87 gave under $10,000 for the year, and their combined giving amounted to only 13.15 percent of the total. Five percent, or 579 churches, gave half of the total foreign-missions giving for the year. Those 579 churches gave $20,000 or more for missions, and of those, 74 gave $100,000 or more.

Doesn't this show how ridiculous is the occasionally heard statement that we are reaching a saturation point in missions giving? There is no shortage of potential missionary money in the Assemblies of God, only a scarcity of vision among pastors and congregations who are not carrying their fair share of the burden of fulfilling the Great Commission.

Sometimes people respond to such figures by saying, "Yes, the big churches give much of the total, but on a per-capita basis the little churches give more." It certainly may be true that many people in small churches give sacrificially and faithfully to missions, but it also is true that 3,973 churches in 1991 gave between zero and $500 for the year. That is one-third of Assemblies of God churches! It is time for the whole Church to respond to the holy claims of Jesus Christ for the whole world.

A Two-Way Street

Communication between missionaries and their supporting churches is a two-way street. Churches continue to send their monthly support, and missionaries report back to the churches with letters and itineration reports. This feedback method has worked very well in those churches and with those missionaries who understand it and are faithful to one another.

Celebrate!

Most missions-minded churches hold some kind of annual emphasis when they raise monthly missionary support and motivate their people to become involved in world evangelism. Many call it their world-missions convention. Although that is an excellent name, it may frighten off some smaller churches who fear the expenses of such an ambitious undertaking. Others call the emphasis a world-missions fair, but this also carries the connotation of a big operation. If a church's plans are too big, people may dread the missions emphasis because of all the work involved. On the other hand, as a church gets bigger it will have more people who are willing to make major commitments and can take on bigger projects.

A New Approach

Why not call the annual missions emphasis a world-missions celebration? That's what it really is, more than a convention or fair. It is a time to celebrate the missionaries who have been supported, the souls that have been saved, and the nations that have been influenced with the gospel through the support and prayers of the church.

The Right Speaker

Missions celebrations may range from a one-Sunday emphasis to a week- or month-long extravaganza. Some churches go all out with missionary parades, departmental booths, banquets, prizes for the best costumes, and much more. At the center of planning for the celebration should be the invitation of missionary speakers. The secret of getting the right speakers is to plan ahead and invite them early. Include both foreign and home missionaries and perhaps your district world-missions director or someone from the national Division of Home or Foreign Missions. Naturally, you will cover all travel expenses and give an honorarium. This is the most expensive part of a missions emphasis, so smaller churches may need to limit themselves to one missionary speaker.

Everyone Gets Involved

The more people you involve in the program the more important it is to set firm dates. If you plan a banquet, put a committee in charge of it. You might ask the Sunday school to plan the parade, the Women's Ministries group to plan the banquet, the Men's Ministries group to build the booths, and the youth group to decorate. Order a theme banner, posters, and other materials from the national offices. You may want to include a missions film or video presentation. Also, promote the event several weeks in advance so that people will look forward to it and participate. Your plans may call for more or less than this, but the key to success will be clear planning and thorough preparation. Know what you want to do, involve other people in the preparation, and then do it. Afterward, consider the strengths and weaknesses of what was done and begin planning for next year.

Go for the Goals

What are the goals of such a missions celebration? Consider the following ideas:

1. Celebrate what the church has done for missions over the past year and affirm the significance of this vital ministry.
2. Communicate with missionaries and allow them to offer their feedback on the success of the program.
3. Motivate the whole congregation and involve people in next year's participation in giving, in prayer, and possibly in evangelism, construction, or other support projects.
4. Raise faith promises for the church's continued world-missions giving for the following year (or 6 months in some churches). Include both youth and children in making faith promises for their age-level missions ministries.
5. Inspire young people to commit themselves to Christian service. Involve children and youth in the planning and presentation of the missions emphasis. Consider planning some special sessions in different rooms designed for youth and children.

Notice that goals for a world-missions celebration include much more than money. The financial support of missionaries is very important, but so are some other considerations. Your annual missions emphasis may be a major factor in guiding young people in their search for God's will in their lives. We must get away from the mistaken concept that if God calls us we become ministers or missionaries, and if He doesn't call us we may do something else.

Lifetime Commitments for Every Christian

Every Christian needs to find God's will for his or her life, regardless of the field of endeavor. For the future, we will need pastors, missionaries, evangelists, Bible college teachers, and others in full-time Christian service. But we will also need dedicated Christian laypeople to support and to be led by those ministers. Every Christian needs to know and to do God's will. Each congregation should see a number of its young people go into full-time Christian ministry, but it should not ignore the spiritual needs of other young people who may feel equally called to other fields. The annual missionary celebration is an excellent time to emphasize lifetime commitments to God and to His service.

Coordinate!

One of the best ways to raise world-missions money is through the faith-promise plan. It is very simple, easy to explain, and so effective that some churches raise their whole budget in this way. The faith-promise plan is said to have originated with Oswald J. Smith, a pastor in Toronto, Canada, who said, "No one has the right to hear the gospel twice until everyone has heard it once." His missions conventions and writings greatly influenced the present methods of raising missionary support in America. We continue to recommend the faith-promise plan because it is the most effective way to raise missionary funds.

Essential Elements of the Faith-Promise Plan

Different churches do their own variations on the faith-promise plan, but the main idea is as follows:

1. Explain to the people that a faith promise is not a pledge but an expression of faith in God to supply their own needs while they support the work of foreign and home missionaries, based on Philippians 4:19. In effect, a person making a faith promise is saying, "God helping me, I will commit myself and my finances to support world missions monthly (or weekly in some churches) for the next year (or 6 months) with this amount." Since it is a goal rather than a pledge, if the person's income should decrease he may adjust his missions giving accordingly. Of course, we should also expect an increase if there is a raise! Many people have testified to increases in their income when they have supported God's primary program.

2. On a Sunday morning during your annual or semiannual missions emphasis, pass out plain 3- by 5-inch cards and ask every family or single person in the church to make a monthly commitment to the church's world-missions ministries. Printed faith-promise cards are available through the national offices, or some churches print their own. Many people prefer the plain cards over the printed ones because they are more informal and less like a contract. All you really need is for people to write their name and the monthly (or weekly) amount that God has laid on their hearts to give regularly to world missions.

3. Have the ushers or missionaries collect the cards and bring them to the pulpit. Some churches count them in the service and announce the result. This is especially exciting if the church has previously set a goal or is using some graphic representation of the giving, such as a thermometer. One church put a globe in a fish tank and poured in a scoop of grain for every $10 promised until the globe was covered. A lot of creativity can go into a faith-promise service. Other churches, particularly those with multiple Sunday morning services, simply receive the cards and announce the results later. Be sure to distinguish between monthly, weekly, and one-time commitments.

4. Teach the people to give their monthly (or weekly) faith promises whenever it is most convenient for them. No special offering needs to be taken. They should just indicate the purpose of the offering by marking "missions" on their envelope. It takes about 3 years to train a congregation to do this, so the pastor must continue to emphasize the faith-promise giving in the bulletin and from the pulpit. Many churches designate the second Sunday of each month as Missions Sunday. Some churches have a poster or a velvet banner that on one side says, "Next Sunday Is Missions Sunday," and on the other says, "Today Is Missions Sunday."

The faith-promise plan works beautifully once it is taught and put into practice—and as long as no one is dunned for his or her faith promise as if it were a pledge.

Faith in Our Father

Something more needs to be said about faith promises. Yes, they are promises, but they are *faith* promises. If people promise only what they know they can pay, no faith is expressed. Faith goes beyond what we can do and moves into the realm of hope. The writer of Hebrews says, "Faith is the substance of things hoped for, the evidence of things not seen" (Hebrews 11:1). We must be realistic and practical, of course, but when we make a faith promise the element of faith must predominate the act. When we put a missionary offering in the plate, it is the substance of what we had hoped to do in the annual missions convention, the evidence of going beyond what we could see before we took that step of faith. God honors such faith and blesses those who so demonstrate their belief in His keeping and sustaining power.

In one faith-promise service, a child wrote on his card, "My father will pay this." It was cute, and the amount was unrealistic, but really that's how we all pay our faith promises. We step out in faith, and our Heavenly Father comes to our rescue.

Some people have wondered why they are asked to put their names on the faith-promise cards if it is a commitment between them and God. In one service a child became very inspired and committed himself to $1,000 a month. The motive was right, but $1 a month would have been closer to his income range. Pastors and missions committees need to know what to expect so they, in turn, may make the church's monthly pledges to the missionaries. Those *are* pledges because the missionaries go out to the foreign fields expecting the church's commitments to continue over the next 4 years and perhaps even throughout their missionary careers.

Cooperate!

One of the main reasons why local churches need to be part of a worldwide fellowship is that no single church can fulfill the Great Commission alone. It takes cooperation and teamwork. One church may support a missionary with $100 a month, but it may take 50 such churches to combine their resources to send that missionary to the mission field. Actually, since much of a missionary's support comes in pledges of $5, $10, $25, and $50, it may take more than 100 churches to raise the budget! Yes, it takes a great amount of cooperation and teamwork. Perhaps a local church gives $20,000 to world missions, but the whole missions program may need more than $100 million that year!

Team churches should try to raise the amounts of their monthly commitments to missionaries and work toward increasing their monthly missions giving. Many pastors feel that a church's world-missions giving should be equal to 10 percent of the church's annual general-fund income. That would mean that a church that received $100,000 in tithes and offerings during the year should give $10,000 or more to missions. Some churches tithe on their general fund, but most raise separate funds equaling a tithe.

We have a big world to evangelize, Jesus is coming soon, and it's now or never for winning the lost.

7
Enlarge Your Circle

There is a wise old saying, usually passed down from parents to their children: If some people draw a circle and leave you out, draw another circle and include them in!

A People Person

By the very nature of faith, Christians must be friendly people, for how we relate to others has much to do with our ability to evangelize the world. Our prime example for interpersonal relations is Jesus Christ himself, whom today's generation might have called a *people Person.* Jesus spent much of His time with people—influencing them for His kingdom, doing good among them, meeting their needs, and never missing an opportunity for a one-on-one conversation. Busy as He was, He always took time to talk personally with people. He met with Nicodemus at night, the Samaritan woman by the well, and the rich young ruler. He attended weddings, accepted dinner invitations, and fed multitudes. He was seen in public places, such as the temple and the pool of Bethesda, and even talked to prostitutes and touched lepers. In Jesus we find the ultimate role model for ministry to the world.

This is what a Christian needs to be; yet the idea of relating to a lot of people runs contrary to the temperament of many individuals. By nature we leave some space between ourselves and most other people. Sociologists say that the average person has no more than five close friends and that many people—especially the immature or insecure—are not capable of having more than one friend at a time. It is common during school years for someone to consider that if you are his or her friend you can have no other friend. How easy it is, then, to draw a circle around our warm little enclave of close acquaintances and leave everyone else out in the cold.

That's the way people are. And yet Jesus told us to go into all the world and preach the gospel of love and salvation to every person—to close friends, to acquaintances, to strangers, and even to those we do not naturally like. We generally appreciate people who are most like ourselves and dislike those who are different from us, but that goes against the calling of God, who "so loved the world, that he gave his only begotten Son" (John 3:16).

Concerned Enough To Care

How, then, are we to get out of our little friendship circles and enlarge our vision to reach the world? As a starting place, we must truly care about the people we come into contact with. If we don't have a burden for the lost—that is, really care about the unchurched and unsaved—then we will never reach out to them to introduce them to the good news of Jesus Christ. Proverbs 18:24 still is true: "A man that hath friends must show himself friendly." We must care, really be concerned, about the condition of lost people. We must realize that they are headed for eternal hell and we must truly care about them. We must carry the gospel personally as our greatest treasure and deliver it with sensitivity and love. Care and carry—that should be the preoccupation of every Christian. But how do we attain it? The answer may by now be obvious: missions education in the local church!

What Do We Mean by Missions?

It may come as a surprise to discover the word *missions* does not appear in the King James Version of the Bible. Why then are we considering missions education in the local church? Or, why should we put so much effort into foreign and home missions?

The singular word *mission* does appear in a few verses in the New International Version (NIV). For example, Joshua 22:3 says, "You . . . have carried out the mission the Lord your God gave you." Most cases have to do with war, such as in 1 Samuel 15:18: "He sent you on a mission, saying, 'Go and completely destroy those wicked people.' "

Deacons and Service

The only NIV use of *mission* in the New Testament is in Acts 12:25: " When Barnabas and Saul had finished their mission, they returned from Jerusalem." The Greek word here is *diakonia* (dee-ah-koh-NEE-ah), usually translated "service" or "ministry." In Acts 21:19 the same word is translated "ministry" in both versions. It comes from the word *diakonos* (dee-AH-koh-nos), from which we get *deacon,* best translated "emphatically a servant." A deacon is one who is especially appointed to serve others. That was why the Early Church appointed deacons to assist the apostles by serving the people (Acts 6:1–7). As the church developed further, deacons served in much the same role to assist the pastors (called "presbyters," "bishops," or "elders"). You may read their qualifications in 1 Timothy 3:8–13.

Our *diakonia* is our ministry, the activity in which we feel most called to serve others. A person might have a music ministry, an ushering ministry, a teaching ministry, or a preaching or pastoral ministry. These individual ministries operate within the greater ministry of every local church, for which the Lord "gave some, apostles; and some, prophets; and some, evangelists; and some, pastors and teachers; for the perfecting of the saints, for the work of the ministry, for the edifying of the body of Christ" (Ephesians 4:11,12). Some call these the five ministries of the Church, but there are more. For example, in 1 Corinthians 12:28 the apostle Paul writes, "God hath set some in the church, first apostles, secondarily prophets, thirdly teachers, after that miracles, then gifts of healings, helps, governments, diversities of tongues." These ministries must be active in churches everywhere and, therefore, do not distinguish the work of local churches from what we call foreign or home missions.

Journeys

It may further surprise you to find that the word *missionary* does not appear in the Bible. Yet, much of the New Testament describes the spread of Christianity, as Jesus foretold in Acts 1:8—from Jerusalem to Judea to Samaria and out to the world. The Book of Acts tells of Stephen's home-missions ministry to the Greek-speaking Synagogue of the Libertines in Jerusalem and of Paul's foreign-missions journeys to Asia Minor, Macedonia, Greece, and Rome. So it is not a question of whether the Bible includes missions but of what word was used for it.

The Early Church had no specific word for it because the whole work of the church was missions. Whether they were ministering in Jerusalem, Judea, Samaria, or out to the other nations, they were doing nothing but missionary work because they were establishing the church in new territories. To ask them about missions would have been like asking a fish about water; the fish would not know how to answer because it has never known anything but water! It was *all* missions in the Early Church.

Apostles and Evangelists

Two New Testament words describe people who moved into new territory for the Lord, "apostles" and "evangelists." The word *apostle* means "one who is sent forth." There were the original apostles, but the Lord also placed the ministry of apostles in the Church. By *missionary,* we mean one who is sent forth on a special mission, so a missionary is a kind of apostle. The word *evangelist* comes from the New Testament word for the gospel, so an evangelist is one who preaches or teaches the gospel to those who have not heard the good news of salvation.

Since the whole work of missionaries is to spread the gospel, a missionary is an evangelist. Paul wrote to the young Timothy, "Endure afflictions, do the work of an evangelist, make full proof of thy ministry" (2 Timothy 4:5). And here once again we encounter the Greek word *diakonia* for "ministry."

For All Churches Everywhere

We have seen, then, that the ministries of Christians are God's gifts for all churches everywhere. There is no essential difference between a church in the United States and one in Nigeria, Singapore, Poland, or Argentina; they all need the full range of Spirit-inspired ministries. What is different about home or foreign missions is that its ministers take the gospel into previously unevangelized territories, foreign countries, and special-need communities, such as the deaf, blind, military, institutional, college, industry, or ethnic groups. Only because some countries have well-established churches and a Christian-related culture do we have any ministries or churches that are considered anything but missionary.

Yet, that very fact may be a problem. Should any church ever stop reaching out to the lost and bringing new converts into the fold? Missions must not be seen as something different from the local church but as a concept that begins in the hearts of the congregation, grows into local evangelization, leads many of its young people into full-time ministry, and sends out missionaries to unevangelized peoples and lands.

How Do We Produce Missionaries?

Missions is not a program but an attitude! It is a way of thinking that is born out of our own personal experience with Jesus Christ, and it grows into a burning passion to share His gospel with everybody everywhere. The missionary outlook comes naturally to people who know Christ as their Savior and have been filled with the Holy Spirit. Jesus said,

> Ye shall receive power, after that the Holy Ghost is come

> upon you: and ye shall be witnesses unto me both in Jerusalem, and in all Judea, and in Samaria, and unto the uttermost part of the earth (Acts 1:8).

The missionary vision develops out of personal Christian experience. It is the natural tendency of Spirit-filled people to be evangelistic. That is why the Pentecostal movement is the fastest-growing element of Christianity all around the world.

Establish a Desire To Grow

If the Pentecostal movement is indeed the fastest-growing element, then why aren't all Pentecostal churches evangelistic and growing? It is a sociological fact that all groups—from stamp-collecting clubs to churches—have a tendency to become stable. Churches grow to certain sizes that seem to meet the needs of the people involved in them and then stop growing. The growth of some churches is limited by the size of their sanctuaries or parking lots, while others are hindered by the scope of their vision.

Many churches are clustered around 35, 85, 125, 180, or 240 in their Sunday morning attendance, and there are few in between those sizes.[1] These are steady numbers that can remain much the same for many years. Once a church becomes stable and enters such a nongrowing mode, it does not engage in much evangelization except for an occasional revival meeting, and even that is intended more to stir up the saints than to reach sinners. In fact, many of the itinerant ministers we call evangelists are not very evangelistic at all, but are revivalists, teachers, seminar directors, or musical performers. They may provide valuable services to the local churches without significantly adding to evangelistic growth.

We may speak of missions education in the local church, but true missions must come from the heart. The entire range of missions-related subjects must be incorporated into the whole program of the church from the nursery to the nursing home. Missions should be constantly emphasized with missionaries coming often to the church and with an annual missions convention. The pastor should preach often on reaching the world for Christ and should lead the way in missionary zeal and missions participation.

Understand the Reality of Heaven and Hell

Yet, many churches that do all these things still fail to produce missionaries out of their own congregation. What may be lacking is the concept that missions is an attitude. It is a particular viewpoint or worldview that sees born-again people as saved and on their way to heaven and all others as lost and going to hell. Jesus said, "He that believeth on the Son hath everlasting life: and he that believeth not the Son shall not see life; but the wrath of God abideth on him" (John 3:36). For those who share this realistic state of mind, the mission field does not begin at the border of a country or an Indian reservation but starts with the unsaved in the congregation, continues beyond the church doors, and moves out through the community, city, county, state, country, continent, and world. Little real difference exists between spreading the gospel across the street or across the seas.

Provide a Setting for Success

If we really want to provide meaningful missions education for our local churches, we must go far beyond teaching about missions and demonstrate the very spirit of missions in all that we do. Our children deserve to grow up in churches where people are being saved at the altars, where congregations are deeply involved in personal witnessing and soul-winning, and where a New Testament atmosphere of praise, prayer, miracles, and deliverance provides a setting for evangelistic efforts to succeed. After all, if Jesus thought He needed miracles and deliverance to get His message across to a sinful world, how do we think we can do it with anything less? Many young missionaries find themselves handicapped on the foreign field because they did not grow up in churches that regularly experienced the supernatural power of God.

Just after Jesus said, "Go ye into all the world, and preach the gospel to every creature" (Mark 16:15), He said that certain signs would accompany true Christian efforts. Evangelistic believers would cast out devils, speak in new tongues, be protected from natural and human dangers, and heal the sick (Mark 16:17,18). This is still the kind of church that will evangelize its own community and reach out to the rest of the world in home and foreign missions. Such a church will produce future missionaries and reproduce itself in kind on the world's mission fields.

How Do We Educate Our People?

If we have the kind of church that should be reproduced on home and foreign mission fields, we must go further to offer a planned and well-integrated program of missions education throughout the congregation.

We have said that by nature people have a limited number of friends. Even Jesus had an inner circle of disciples—Peter, James, and John. Outside their "insider" group of close friends, people have a larger circle of acquaintances who are bound together by some common bond such as a family, a neighborhood, or a church. In larger churches, people associate themselves with smaller groups within the congregation, such as home Bible study groups, Sunday school classes, or church ball teams. Beyond this level, they have an even larger circle of people with whom they have something in common, such as being part of a whole congregation or a community. Thus, people's identification is established in concentric circles from themselves to friends they know best to people they know least. A believer might see himself or herself as an individual, a part of a group of friends, a church member, a city resident, an American, and a member of the human race. We must add to those factors such elements of personal identity as gender, race, language, and culture.

Take Time To Talk

The problem is that we tend to talk with our friends and

others with whom we most closely identify ourselves. That is why sometimes new people in a church complain that no one talks to them. It isn't really that the congregation doesn't like them, but that each person talks with his or her own friends and feels no particular responsibility to open conversation with a stranger. Even in churches considered to be friendly, the greeting of visitors will be done by a minority of the congregation.

World missions must start at home. A missions-minded church will begin its worldwide campaign with its own people and community. As we educate our congregations to care about people outside their own circles of friends and acquaintances, we provide an environment that will bring about church growth and produce future missionaries.

Right Attitudes Precede Right Actions

What a church *is* will result in what it *does.* Right attitudes lead to right activities, so a missions program will derive out of the hearts of a caring and loving congregation. The church itself and every department of the church will continue to relate to the church's threefold purpose of worshiping God, caring for the congregation, and reaching out to the lost.

Creating an Effective Missions Program

Let us suppose, for the sake of simplicity, that a minister becomes the pastor of a church that never has involved itself in world missions. No missionaries have spoken in the church, there are no missions-related programs or activities, and the church is on that list of 17 percent of Assemblies of God churches that give nothing to missions. As a qualified and well-trained man or woman of God, the pastor recognizes that the church has been out of God's will and that the development of an effective world-missions program must be a high priority over the following months. (The blame for any church's being in such a sad condition would have to be placed on the former pastor, whose duty it should have been to lead the congregation in God's ways. Local congregations seldom resist normal missionary ministries.)

Initial Strategies

The pastor should begin his or her campaign by preaching on the Great Commission. This foundation of missions thinking should be followed on a regular basis by sermons on salvation, soul-winning, and caring about the condition of others. Generally, a church that often has souls saved in its own community will also develop a greater world vision. The pastor should follow up his or her preaching by bringing in missionary speakers to inspire the people and involve them in giving to missions. Some pastors use BGMC to establish monthly giving to missions and, as funds increase, they set up a separate missions fund and begin to send monthly support for missionaries of their choice. In the Assemblies of God, foreign-missions support is mailed to the Division of Foreign Missions at the International Headquarters in Springfield, Missouri, and designated for foreign, home, Boys and Girls Missionary Crusade, Speed–the–Light, Light–for–the–Lost, or Women's Ministries accounts. Some kinds of home-missions support is sent to the Division of Home Missions, and other such support goes to the district office.

A church that has reached this level of involvement is already well on its way to becoming a missions-minded church. In fact, the pastor may be surprised at how quickly and easily a church becomes enthusiastic about evangelizing the world. Reaching out to others is the natural state of the church; it is the isolationist church that is unnatural and stunted in its growth.

An Annual Convention

Next, the pastor should initiate an annual world-missions convention to celebrate the accomplishments of the congregation and to lift up the people's eyes to the future. This would be the time to introduce the faith-promise plan of missions giving in which each person in the church writes his or her personal goal for missions giving on a card. The individual faith promises add up to the annual or semiannual goal of the whole church. It takes about 3 years for this plan to be established. The church may go all out with decorations, a parade, booths, and a banquet, or it may just invite a missionary speaker and collect faith promises at the end of a Sunday morning service. The church needs some kind of annual emphasis to educate and inspire the people, raise money, and stimulate prayer. And, of course, the church should include the missionary speaker in the monthly support he or she helps to raise!

Follow-Up Education Strategies

The wise pastor knows that anything gained by preaching or promotion can decline again as quickly at it was gained. When a person responds to an altar call to accept Christ as Savior, the church must incorporate that person into the church and offer continued instruction. The follow-up of new converts is every bit as important as whatever brought them to Christ in the first place. Similarly, to have a truly missionary-minded church it is not enough to hear missions speakers and to support missionaries. There must be missions education throughout the congregation from the youngest to the oldest members. It is not enough to spread the gospel; it must also be established in depth. Like the crosspieces of the cross, the gospel must be planted both horizontally and vertically, both in breadth and in depth.

The Assemblies of God offers a variety of missions- and age-related ministries. It is a mistake for a pastor to see them as options; they should, rather, be considered as an integrated single environment for missions education in the local church. It would make no sense to have a program for the children and then fail to continue the emphasis among the teenagers or young adults.

In the Assemblies of God, an integrated missions program will include Boys and Girls Missionary Crusade for children,

Speed–the–Light and Ambassadors in Mission for young people, Missions Abroad Placement Service and Missionary in Training for adults, Women's Ministries for women, Light–for–the–Lost for men, and itinerating missionaries and missions conventions for the whole church. This is the package, a single package for an integrated world-missions program.

Boys and Girls Missionary Crusade

Boys and Girls Missionary Crusade provides educational material for Sunday school and/or children's church to train children in missions-giving and to educate them about how a Christian views and deals with the world. In a brochure titled "Have a Heart for BGMC," the Sunday School Department says,

> The Boys and Girls Missionary Crusade, BGMC, is a missions education program dedicated to teaching children about the world's need for salvation. BGMC opens children's eyes to colorful cultures in faraway lands and special needs of people all across the earth. Best of all, BGMC trains children to respond to the Great Commission—personally! Since its inception in 1949, BGMC has worked to spread the gospel by providing all sorts of printed materials for our missionaries. Pennies, nickels, dimes, and dollars given by caring children add up to nearly $2 million annually.

Speed–the–Light

Speed–the–Light is a missions program of the national Youth Department, which raises more than $4.5 million annually to provide transportation and communication equipment for evangelism worldwide. Children raised on BGMC will quite naturally continue in their teenage years to be personally involved in STL by giving $2 a week in faith promises and by raising money through car washes, rocking chair rock-a-thons, rallies, and other creative activities. Only eternity will reveal the great advantage given Assemblies of God missionaries because of this program.

Much of the STL work is coordinated through the district

offices and is a major part of the work of local youth ministers. Many young adults continue to support BGMC and STL even while involving themselves in the whole missions ministry of the church. Furthermore, people raised on these programs will encourage their own children and will help lead and teach in the programs.

Short-Term Missionary Service

Some young adults take 2 or 3 years out of their own career plans to go into short-term missionary service through MAPS. There are two versions of the program. The foreign program, Ministries Abroad Placement Service, places secretaries, teachers, builders, and people with many other occupations on foreign fields to help the missionaries for limited-time periods of ministry. These volunteers are supported by their own savings or by family, friends, and local churches. The program especially appeals to both youth and retired adults. The home-missions version of MAPS is called Mission America Placement Service.

Maintain Balanced Ministries

By establishing such an integrated program in the local church, the pastor produces a proper balance in the ministry of the church and brings it into obedience to the commands of the Lord Jesus Christ.

We began this chapter with a common saying about including other people in our circle of friends. A missions-minded church constantly seeks ways to enlarge its circle. On the cross, Jesus spread out His arms to the world, and His most dedicated people today do the same, no matter how great the sacrifice.

---

[1]David A. Womack, *The Pyramid Principle of Church Growth* (Minneapolis: Bethany Fellowship, 1977), 17.

8
A Missions-Friendly Environment

One of the most difficult problems for foreign missionaries is what to do about their children. Preachers' kids are called PKs; missionaries' kids are MKs. Some families choose to educate their own children with correspondence courses; others in major cities enroll their children in English language schools used by embassy families and other expatriate Americans; some must send their children away to boarding schools for months at a time; and a few put their children in the national schools. The amazing and probably miraculous truth is that in spite of sacrifices, hard work, and loneliness, MKs tend to turn out very well. They enjoy the advantages of being intercultural people, speaking two or more languages, having a fine record of accomplishments, and often going on to become missionaries themselves. It is not a handicap to be an MK!

Some missionary kids like to say, "Our parents were called to be missionaries, but we were drafted!"

Church people often think they should feel sorry for them, but it is hard to find an MK who does not love the country of his or her parents' calling. Most say they miss the native food and can hardly wait to get back to the foreign field to see their friends again. They have fond memories of growing up overseas and may even feel out of place among people who do not know the world as well as they do.

The Division of Foreign Missions provides a number of special services for missionaries' children, especially for older ones who may remain in America to finish high school or to go to college. Some districts hold annual retreats for MKs and PKs.

Since so many missionary children enjoy foreign life, we should help our church children share in the joy of world missions. We often present the missionary challenge in our most serious tones and with great intensity, but we also need to allow our people, particularly our children, to experience the fact that missions can be fun. We want them to feel good about world missions and to make lifelong commitments to the global cause of Jesus Christ.

Let's Get Creative!

We expect to find certain programs in every Christian, evangelical, Pentecostal church. By "Christian" we mean two things—both that we belong to the whole broad spectrum of the Christian religion and, more specifically, that we follow the teachings of Jesus Christ. When people use the word *Christian* we must know if they mean all who say they are Christians or only those who truly live the Christian life.

By "evangelical" we mean those churches that are committed to preaching the gospel and bringing people to an experience of salvation through the blood of Jesus Christ. The term is generally used only for individuals or groups who believe the Bible is the infallible (without error) Word of God.

By "Pentecostal" we mean those churches whose people identify themselves with the beliefs, experiences, practices, and priorities of the original Church born on the Day of Pentecost. Thus, by calling ourselves Pentecostal we go from the most general description to the most specific definition. We believe that true Christianity is original Christianity as demonstrated and taught by our Lord and by His first followers, beginning on the Day of Pentecost.

Pentecostals Are Creative People

Pentecostal Christianity is whole Christianity, or what we sometimes call "full gospel," by which we mean that we leave out nothing of the fullness of New Testament Christian life and experience. Our most distinctive difference from other churches is that, like the first Christians, we believe that people who are filled with the Holy Spirit will speak in other tongues. Acts 2:4 says the first Christians "were all filled with the Holy Ghost, and began to speak with other tongues, as the Spirit gave them utterance." That same day, Peter preached the first Christian sermon and ended by saying of the baptism in the Holy Spirit, "The promise is unto you, and to your children, and to all that are afar off, even as many as the Lord our God shall call" (Acts 2:39). That is, the baptism in the Holy Spirit with speaking in other tongues would be for that generation, the next generation, and for all future generations that the Lord would call to salvation.

To be baptized in the Holy Spirit is to be filled with the very Spirit of the Creator, so Pentecostal Christians ought to be the most creative people in the world. We should not fear new ways of doing things. In fact, it is at our moments of inspiration, or what we call "the anointing," that we are at our Christian best. It makes no sense at all for a Pentecostal church to be conservative in its style or ministry; we ought to be people who are constantly breaking new ground and doing new things for God.

We assume that a Pentecostal church will be thoroughly Christian, completely evangelical in outlook and action, and fully Pentecostal in emphasis and experience. We expect to find lively, celebration-style services because we are worshiping in the presence of the living God, not holding formal ceremonies in memory of traditional truths or historical happenings. We presume that a Pentecostal church will have a Sunday school, services on Sunday morning and Sunday night and at least one night during the week, an active youth group, midweek children's ministries, and other such programs. When people move to a new community, they expect to find such programs and will search from one church to another until they find one that meets their needs and expectations. Is having such programs a contradiction to our creativity? No, being creative does not mean we do not do some basic things well.

SOCIAL PATTERNS REQUIRE CREATIVE RESPONSES

We must accept, however, that as social patterns change, some churches will change to meet the new needs. Some churches have moved their "Sunday" school to Saturday and claim they are reaching more children. New York has been called "the city that never sleeps," but more and more cities have people awake and working at all hours of the day and night. A church in Las Vegas holds a service at 1 o'clock on Monday morning! A church in Oakland, California, started a clown ministry and takes its "Sunday" school to the streets and parks all through the week. Pentecostal Christians are the ultimate opportunists who take advantage of any opening to present the gospel of Jesus Christ to a lost world.

Holding missionary services is a fundamental fact of life in most Pentecostal churches because a missionary vision is basic to our beliefs.

MISSIONARY SERVICES DEMAND CREATIVITY

We believe in missions, and we love missionaries. Yet, we do not always love missionary services because they are predictable fund-raising events. We need to apply our most inspired creativity to these important services.

The best missionary services are often those in which the missionary does what he or she does on the mission field, rather than just telling what he or she did or giving a travelogue. Let people be saved, filled with the Holy Spirit, healed, or delivered in a missionary service, and we'll probably support that missionary for the rest of his or her career.

Typically, an itinerating missionary arrives for a service, attempts to meet with the pastor before church, sets up some sort of display, and makes prayer cards available so people will not forget his or her name and face. In the service, after songs and prayer, the missionary usually introduces himself and his family, tells about his field and work, and preaches. At the end of the service, the pastor takes up a missionary offering, and the missionary leaves a monthly pledge form with the pastor in hope that the church will include him or her on its monthly support list. It's over, and the missionary is gone—except for a few follow-up calls to try to prod the pastor into action. Missionaries know that the pastor is the key for most missionary support and that excuses such as "The committee hasn't met yet" are procrastinations if not rejections.

Creative Financial Support

Of course, a church will not offer its monthly support to every missionary who comes, but quite often will give missionaries a good offering and send them on their way. Many churches have a minimum amount they will give so that even if attendance is down the missionary will be blessed. Consider making the amount of the church's minimum missionary offering equal to the Sunday morning church attendance. That is, a church that runs 100 in its morning services would never give a missionary less than $100, or a church of 300 would set a $300 minimum. Of course, that would not be the maximum!

We must give the missionaries everything that is raised in their name. If the people think they are giving an offering for Missionary Jones, then the whole offering must go to Missionary Jones. If every church would follow these two principles—setting a minimum for missionary offerings and giving the missionary all that comes in for him or her—we could significantly speed up the itineration process and get the missionaries back to the field sooner.

Creative Fellowship and Planning

One of the needs of missionaries is to meet with the pastor before the service. This makes for better planning and better missionary services. If a missionary will be speaking in a Sunday night or midweek service, the pastor should ask the missionary to arrive early to share a meal, to get acquainted, and to plan the service. It is in the pastor's best interests, as well as the missionary's, to increase the effectiveness and interest level of missionary services. If the missionary will be coming for a Sunday morning service, the pastor should invite him or her to arrive on Saturday and to meet together for the Saturday night meal. The church should put the missionary up for the night and provide breakfast and Sunday dinner. With all the stresses of missionary itineration, missionaries really appreciate being put up in a good motel or hotel instead of in a private home where they must sit up late talking with strangers.

Pastors who say they do not have time for fellowship with itinerating missionaries are missing an important contribution to their own lives from some of God's most dedicated men and women. They must come to realize that missionaries can do a better job of missions education and inspiration in a church where the pastor has shown personal interest in them. And some young pastors have received their own call to foreign missions after a good, long talk with a missionary.

Involve People Creatively

Many pastors have experienced the sad fact that attendance often goes down when they announce a missionary service. This particularly happens in churches where there is no integrated plan of missions education and the pastor does not preach regularly on missions and evangelism. The congregation is apt to see the service only in terms of fund-raising and promotion.

The solution is to become more creative with missionary services and to involve more people in the process. For example, the chairman of the World Missions Committee should be on the platform and have a part in the service. A youth representative should be there to talk with the missionary after the service about his or her use of a Speed–the–Light vehicle and to take a report back to the youth group. The BGMC coordinator, the Sunday school superintendent, or a designated person from the Sunday school should ask about the literature the missionary has used from the Boys and Girls Missionary Crusade. The men should ask about the evangelistic literature provided by Light–for–the–Lost. The women need to know how their projects have benefited the missionary. Missionettes and

Royal Rangers may have questions about their involvements in missions. A missionary service needs to be a dynamic exchange between the missionary and the congregation. Of course, we are limited by time and people's schedules, but the creative church will find ways to enhance its missionary services.

TRY A FEW NEW IDEAS

To put more life into your missionary services, discuss your plans with the missionary in advance and try some of the following ideas:

1. If the missionary is going to be with you for a Sunday morning, plan a Saturday evening event with the world-missions coordinator and people from the various departments. The informal discussion in such a meeting will do wonders for the church program and increase participation in Boys and Girls Missionary Crusade, Speed–the–Light, Light–for–the–Lost, Women's Ministries, Men's Ministries, and other programs.

2. Involve the Sunday school. Have the missionary visit each department or class. Or have him or her teach an adult class or a combined class on missions. One missionary, after preaching in two morning services and being taken from class to class in the Sunday school, said, "I feel like I've preached three services." No, more than that! Each class was a separate and important challenge. Work those missionaries; they'll love it (especially if you support them).

3. Allow the missionary to leave the platform temporarily to pay a visit to the children's church.

4. At the Sunday meal, or after church Sunday night, include the world-missions coordinator and others involved with your missions leadership.

5. For a Sunday night service, include an interview with the missionary to bring out information of interest to the congregation. People want to know their missions giving is effective and is being well-spent. Of course, allow for motivational preaching in every missionary service! In a Pentecostal church

the Sunday night service should be the most inspirational and motivational meeting of the week. In growing churches with two morning services, the Sunday night service may be the largest single gathering in the church. Missionaries must be alert and well-prepared for these services if they want pastors to continue to invite missionaries for Sunday nights.

6. Midweek services often are highly structured meetings with simultaneous adult and children's ministries in different parts of the building. When you have a missionary who is skilled in ministering to children, bring the children into the missionary service, or have someone escort the missionary around to the different groups during the first part of the service.

7. Not every missionary is a strong pulpiteer, but each one has something important to contribute to the vision and scope of the church. Rather than declining to invite a missionary to a Sunday morning service, allow 20 minutes for the missionary's presentation and involve him or her in the Sunday school. It is often better for the missionary to have a shorter time on Sunday morning than a longer time in a less-attended midweek service. Generally, the larger the church the less likely it is that a missionary will be given the whole Sunday morning service. And yet, a large part of the overall world-missions giving comes from those larger churches. Missionaries should not be offended when asked to take only a part of a service, for they will reach many more people in those 20 minutes than by holding whole services with fewer potential supporters.

Be Open to New Methods

There are many more ways to improve the communication between missionaries and their supporting churches, but these will perhaps spark your imagination and creativity. Due to the shortage of time in regular missionary services, each church needs to carry out a well-planned annual missions convention that will include speaking events, perhaps a potluck meal of international foods, and plenty of opportunities for dialogue with the missionaries.

Missions in the Classroom

Every Sunday school teacher knows that kids say the most unpredictable things. One little girl who had memorized the books of the Bible was repeating them for her pastor. When she came to Ecclesiastes, she said, "Easy Elastees." Another girl who had learned in Sunday school to sing "Gimme That Old Time Religion" came home singing, "It was good for 'pendicitis, and it's good enough for me." It took some time for her mother to discover that she meant, "It was good for Paul and Silas." And for another child the complicated line "Gladly the cross I'll bear" came out "Gladly the cross-eyed bear."

In a missionary service, a pastor asked the children, "What is a missionary?" One boy raised his hand and replied, "A missionary is a girl!" After an awkward silence, the people began to laugh as they realized he had confused "missionary" with "Missionette" (a girl in the Missionettes program). A mother asked her little daughter, "Honey, what is a missionary?" Without hesitation, the girl replied, "A missionary is a thing that goes *mish!*"

Well, rather than allowing our missionaries to "go *mish,*" we must give serious thought to how we communicate world missions to our little people. Three things need to happen for good missions education among children.

1. Children need to hear about missionaries in a positive role-developing way. People who win others to Christ should be commended, and any child who brings someone new to church should be congratulated. An Assemblies of God Sunday school needs the BGMC program to provide free monthly missions-education materials and Buddy Barrels and to offer a practical and enjoyable outlet for children's missions giving.

2. Children need to meet missionaries. After a missionary service, parents should introduce their children to the missionary. If possible, the missionary should be brought to the

classrooms and introduced to the students. (Children may be caught off guard by having a missionary suddenly brought into their classroom and will not know what to say or ask. Teachers should tell them in advance that the missionary will be coming so they may be prepared and not be embarrassed to ask questions.)

3. Children need to develop a healthy worldview. Think about how children view the outside world, the world beyond their personal experience. Many parents have the television news on during meals. In fact, those programs are designed to catch people during mealtimes. That means children will see the outside world as filled with violence, wars, crime, and immorality. Yes, there are some great documentaries on positive things in the world, but children are not apt to watch the educational channels. Rather, they watch some demonic force trying to take over the world in the Saturday morning cartoons! That is the world in which our children live and which forms their concepts and sense of any personal responsibility about the world. How important it is that children learn that "God so loved the world, that he gave . . . ." We must help our children escape the trap of being provincial in their thinking or of being unrealistic about the true state of the world.

Many people have never traveled more than a few miles from their home, so their worldview is limited to the little portion that they know. One man who lived near the Canadian border in Washington but had never crossed it said, "We have everything we need right here. We have mountains, deserts, lakes, and ocean beaches. Why should we go anywhere else?" Other people might point out that getting snowed in every winter might not appeal to everyone.

Such provincial thinking that once characterized nearly everyone in our country is now becoming rare as people travel more, are better educated, and are exposed to the electronic media. Today's American children have the opportunity to develop a more comprehensive worldview than that of their parents because of their social environment and the sheer amount of world data flowing to them via education and television. Yet we must be concerned about the quality of the information coming to them.

It is not at all unusual today for our children to attend school with boys and girls who are socially, culturally, ethnically, or linguistically different from themselves. America has always been a nation of immigrants, and this time-honored tradition continues. Everybody in America came here from somewhere. Even the Indians, who sometimes prefer to be called Native Americans, came from the Old World through Alaska or by sea. Many of them suffered greatly at the hands of the Spanish conquistadors and English settlers when they arrived. African Americans whose ancestors were first brought to the New World as slaves now are a vital part of American life and culture.

In the 19th century, teams of Irish immigrants and Civil War veterans built the transcontinental railroad from the East, while Chinese workers built the railroad from the West, until the two met at Promontory Point, Utah, on May 10, 1869, and drove in the Golden Spike. Both the Irish and the Chinese suffered the effects of prejudice and persecution, and yet both are important elements in American culture today.

Spanish-speaking people are quick to point out that the Spanish language was spoken in the Americas long before the first word of English was heard in these lands. In fact, the Spanish already had established universities in the New World when the Pilgrims landed at Plymouth Rock. The more recently arrived Vietnamese, Cambodians, Iranians, Mexicans, Central Americans, and others also are making important contributions to our American culture.

Just a few years ago, included in the *Pentecostal Evangel's* foreign-missions pages was an article with pictures of little missionary children playing with African boys and girls. Twenty people or churches canceled their subscriptions to the denominational magazine because of that! With whom did they think that missionaries' kids play? Very few missionaries' children have married foreigners (not that it's anybody's business). But both missionaries and their children are intercultural people with many friends from outside their own cultural enclave.

If we really intend to evangelize the world, as Jesus Christ told us to do in the Great Commission, we must teach our children to set aside provincial prejudices and to learn to live in a multicultural and constantly blending world. Some parents object that if their sons and daughters play with Vietnamese-American children they may become Buddhists, that Iranian-American children may convince them to become Muslims, or that Mexican-American friends may cause them to become Roman Catholics. The truth is that immigrants often have a hard time relating their old religion to life in America and are much more influenced by their contacts with us. Jesus said, "Go ye into all the world" (Mark 16:15). Yes, our children are going to be influenced by their intercultural contacts; however, conversion to other religions seldom happens. It also is true that some of our children are adversely influenced by the ungodliness of people of their own culture!

Intercultural friendships enrich our lives and make it possible for us to fulfill the task of the Great Commission. All missionaries have to be intercultural people, and we must encourage intercultural friendships if we are to encourage our children to become missionaries.

A Missions Environment

These days we speak often of things that are damaging our environment. Our children are especially aware of the problem because of the discussion of such issues on television and in the public schools. Parents who saw spewing smokestacks as a sign of technological progress now are faced with children who are horrified at the sight of air pollution.

Our living environment—the air we breathe, the water we drink, the food we eat—is so threatened today that the very survival of the human race is at risk.

The question of environment includes both positive and negative elements. For example, we want a good balance of oxygen and carbon dioxide in our atmosphere, but we abhor cancer-causing chemicals, acid rain, and the damage to our ozone layer. Christians must become involved in such issues because in the first chapter of the Bible God told us to manage this earth (Genesis 1:27–29). If we don't care for the physical environment, many people will die; however, if we don't do something about the spiritual environment, people will face eternal damnation in hell!

Someone said, "The problem around here is apathy—but who cares?" No Christian can afford to be apathetic about world missions.

We must ask the question, How may we provide a healthy environment that will encourage everyone in the family to respond positively and generously to world evangelism? The following are a few suggestions:

1. The pastor should preach often on witnessing, soul-winning, and world missions, for the pastor is the number one role model for the church. He should invite missionaries to speak often in the church and include an annual world-missions convention in his or her plans. Since a church's lack of missionary interest is directly attributable to the pastor, some churches send their pastors on overseas preaching trips to assure themselves of his or her continuing world vision. Most missions-minded churches will have some sort of display to keep their missionaries and projects before the people.

2. Sunday school teachers, Missionettes sponsors, and Royal Rangers leaders should put up decorations, posters, and other materials in the classroom to constantly keep the world and its peoples before the students. A world map or globe would be a good teaching resource. Some classes emphasize a missionary-of-the-month and display a picture or a map of the mission field and some information about the missionary's work and family.

3. Throughout the church an emphasis should be placed on the congregation's worldwide interests and concerns. Excellent posters, banners, world flags, and other materials are available from the national offices. Teachers of all classes should be informed about missions and instructed to speak often about mis-

sions and the need to reach the world for Christ. Teachers can sometimes get international posters from airlines or travel agencies.

4. Exposure to other cultures should be a regular part of the church's missions-education curriculum. This may take many forms, ranging from talking positively about people of other cultures to inviting foreigners to the church. Let us not forget that the Bible itself is the single most important exposure to other cultures in the church. How can we understand the Bible if we do not study the cultures of Samaria, Canaan, Egypt, Assyria, Babylonia, or Israel? Suprising as it may seem, no one in the Bible ever spoke English, read the King James Version of the Bible, or tasted pizza! In fact, no one in the Bible ever saw the whole Bible in one book, and it is unlikely that anyone in the first century ever saw all the books of the New Testament. The gospel began among Aramaic-speaking Jews in Palestine and spread to Greek-speaking people in Syria, Galatia, Asia Minor, Macedonia, Greece, and the world. Intercultural contact has been at the heart of Christianity since the very beginning.

5. The church should participate in an annual world-missions convention to educate the congregation and to raise missions funds.

6. The church should participate in the faith-promise plan to support missions on a monthly basis. This approach is not only for the adults, but also for all the children and young people. A child who makes a monthly commitment of 25¢ today will someday give $25 or $250 a month to reach the world.

7. The church should participate in the Boys and Girls Missionary Crusade program. BGMC is one of the best tools for missions education for children. The free monthly materials available from the Sunday School Promotion and Training Department provide an excellent format for training in missions and give the children an easy-to-understand way to get personally involved and to share their money with missionaries.

The hero of BGMC is Buddy Barrel. Because missionaries

often ship their supplies in steel drums, Buddy Barrel is a barrel with arms, legs, and a face. Children who participate in BGMC are given little barrel banks in which to save their coins for the BGMC offering, which goes to the missionaries for evangelism and educational literature. Pencil Pal encourages the children to pray for and to write to missionaries. Winnie the World teaches the children to love the world as God loves the world. She is featured on a weekly-reader type page and shares an ethnic recipe each month.

Many churches use creative ways to promote interest in missions through BGMC. Some have an ongoing competition between the boys and the girls to see who gives the most for missions. Some make a life-sized, full-body costume of Buddy Barrel and have him make regular visits to report on how BGMC money was spent. Other churches make a Buddy Barrel out of a real barrel and have someone in a back room speak for Buddy over the church's sound system. With a little creativity, BGMC can be a lot of fun for children and adults.

Another great idea is to print all-star missionary trading cards like those children (and adults) collect of their favorite sports figures. These provide a fun way to learn about Assemblies of God pioneer missionaries and those currently serving on the field. They also help to pass along our great missions heritage to a new generation of kids.

The whole world-missions program can be enjoyable for adults, young people, and children if pastors and their people will care about reaching the lost and will be creative in their local church missions education.

9

Finding Meaning in Missions

Have you ever wished you could have a face-to-face conversation with Jesus? Yes, we can do that through prayer, but what if He were to walk into your room and you could ask Him your most important questions?

You might be like Thomas who was full of questions about the resurrected Lord until Jesus himself appeared in the room, and then Thomas declared, "My Lord and my God" (John 20:28). There is every evidence in the Gospels that Jesus encouraged questions so He could give answers about the most perplexing problems of life. The disciples had such an experience in John 13:36 through 14:31.

A Little Talk With Jesus

Jesus had been talking about going away, so Peter asked Him, "Lord, whither goest thou?" (John 13:36). It was a reasonable question that any of us might have asked. Jesus replied, "Whither I go, thou canst not follow me now; but thou shalt follow me afterward" (13:36). It was a simple question and answer, but in it Jesus taught that He would ascend into heaven while the Church would remain in the world for a while. That is still the condition of the Church; we are in the world, and Jesus is with the Father in heaven.

That answer didn't satisfy Peter, so he insisted, "Lord, why cannot I follow thee now?" (13:37). Jesus' answer takes up the last verses of John 13 and the first four verses of chapter 14. He promised that He would come again to take His church to heaven but said there would be two reasons for the delay. First, He had to get the Church ready for heaven; and, second, He had to get heaven ready for the Church. Peter would deny the Lord three times, so he wasn't ready to go. Furthermore, Jesus said, "I go to prepare a place for you" (14:2). Just think how beautiful heaven must be after all these years of preparing it for us! Jesus ended by saying, "And whither I go ye know, and the way ye know" (14:4).

This was one of those hey-wait-a-minute moments. Thomas, always thinking and seeking the truth, said, "Lord, we know not whither thou goest; and how can we know the way?" (14:4). Jesus had just taken him further than his mind could thus far conceive (something the Lord always does with His most fervent seekers). It gave Jesus the occasion to say some of the most beautiful words in the whole Bible: "I am the way, the truth, and the life" (14:6).

The Only Way

Every religion seems to have its version of a way or path to some sought-for experience; for example, the Buddhists have their Path of Enlightenment. Jesus fulfilled all religion when He declared that He is the way or path to God. Philosophy asks questions such as "What is the nature of reality?" Philosophy seeks to know what is true. Jesus answered the questions of philosophy by saying He is the truth. Every question ultimately leads to God.

One astronomer said, "The universe is looking more and more like a great thought." Science seeks the secrets of life, from how it may be maintained to how it started in the first place. Jesus said He is the life. John wrote, "All things were made by him; and without him was not any thing made that was made. In him was life; and the life was the light of men" (John 1:3,4). He is the very Source of life, the Creator of life. Our whole hope of eternal life is based on who Jesus is and what He did for us by His life, death, and resurrection.

Jesus then went on to make a shocking statement. "No man

cometh unto the Father, but by me" (John 14:6). Jesus was saying that all human religions are false and that we can come to the one true God only through Him.

The disciples were mystified by Jesus' teachings about heaven, but this statement struck right to the heart of earth. There is no more sensitive subject in the world than whether people's religion is true. We can imagine the disciples' silence as they considered the implications of Jesus' statement. For them it meant that the Jewish religion was wrong or at best only an early stage in God's revelation to mankind. It meant that the Greeks and Romans were wrong about their many gods. For us today, it means that the Muslims, the Buddhists, the Hindus, the Shintoists, the Confucianists, the animists, the cultists, and those of all other religions are wrong. Other religions are the result of mankind's seeking God; Christianity is God's seeking mankind.

Because Jesus Christ had relatively few followers at the time, for the disciples, Jesus' statement meant that only they were right and the rest of the world was wrong. Yet this is ever the way with change. Eugene Debs (1855–1926) wrote, "When great changes occur in history, when great principles are involved, as a rule the majority are wrong."

Doubts Answered

The usually quiet Philip said, "Lord, show us the Father, and it sufficeth us" (John 14:8). No doubt, he was thinking there was no way Jesus could be right. How could all the world be wrong and only those few people possess the truth? For the disciples to believe that Jesus was the only way to God, He would have to show God to them. It may seem presumptuous to us now, but at the time Philip had to challenge Jesus' shocking statement.

In the next 13 verses, Jesus gave him a three-part answer that apparently satisfied the disciples.

Answer #1: Jesus' Revelation of the Father

Jesus asked, "Have I been so long time with you, and yet

hast thou not known me, Philip? he that hath seen me hath seen the Father; and how sayest thou then, Show us the Father?" (14:9). The fact was that He had been showing them the Father all the time. Jesus was in the Father, and the Father was in Him. Even the words that He spoke He did not speak of himself; they were the expressions of the Father. Therefore, Jesus said, "Believe me that I am in the Father, and the Father in me: or else believe me for the very works' sake" (14:11). His first line of defense in proving He was showing them the Father was the works or miracles that He had done, for no one but God could have performed the acts the disciples had seen Him do.

Many years after this conversation, the apostle John wrote in the first chapter of his Gospel that Jesus, the Word of God or the Messiah, was the very Creator of the world ("All things were made by him" [John 1:3]), and that "the Word was made flesh, and dwelt among us, (and we beheld his glory, the glory as of the only begotten of the Father,) full of grace and truth" (John 1:14). We call this the Incarnation, in which God himself "was made flesh, and dwelt among us." So Jesus really is the only way to God because He is God! Only He could show anyone the Father. Jesus' first argument was the proof of His own Person.

But what about all of us who were not there with Philip and the other disciples to see Jesus' works and take that leap of faith without personal experience? In a later conversation, Jesus said to Thomas, "Because thou hast seen me, thou hast believed: blessed are they that have not seen, and yet have believed" (John 20:29). For all of us who were not there with the first disciples, Jesus offered two more proofs of His ability to show us the Father.

Answer #2: Answered Prayer

As His second proof, Jesus gave us the promise of answered prayer. He said, "Whatsoever ye shall ask in my name, that will I do, that the Father may be glorified in the Son. If ye shall ask any thing in my name, I will do it" (John 14:13,14). So active would be His responses to prayer that the works that He did we may do also, and even greater in number. So His second proof was answered prayer.

Answer #3: The Baptism in the Holy Spirit

For the third proof of His person and power, Jesus began with a special requirement: "If ye love me, keep my commandments" (John 14:15). A life of love for Jesus Christ and holy obedience to His teachings would be required to understand this third proof.

In the Old Testament tabernacle, the general population could not see much beyond the outer fence that encircled the holy compound. Those who entered through the *one gate* (symbolic of Jesus Christ as the only way to God) could see only the *brazen altar* (salvation through the blood of the sacrificed lamb), the *laver* (baptism in water), and the *outer coverings* of the tabernacle itself. The *priests who entered* into the *Holy Place* (symbolic of the inner life in the Spirit) could see only the *golden candlestick* (the baptism in the Holy Spirit) on their left, the *altar of incense* (continuous prayer) before them, and the *table of showbread* (the nourishment of the Word of God) on their right. And only the high priest once a year could go past the inner veil into the *hidden Holy of Holies* (the pure presence of God) and see the ark of the covenant with its *tablets of the Law* (obedience), *bowl of manna* (sustenance), and *Aaron's rod that budded* (authority to do miracles), and the *golden mercy seat* with its cherubim (the very throne of God). At every level of spiritual development, no one could see past his own stage of progress.

This principle becomes a major problem in telling people who Jesus is or what He can do in their lives. The unevangelized are totally blinded to Him and often must see miracles of healing and deliverance before they can believe, just as the disciples did. That is why without the supernatural it will be impossible to evangelize the world. A missions-minded church must also be a powerful supernatural church that is known for its love for Jesus Christ and its answered prayers.

The third proof of Jesus' ability to show us the Father will be understood only by those who already love Jesus and live holy lives according to His commandments. That third proof is the *baptism in the Holy Spirit.* Jesus said we would know who He was by the presently powerful working of the Holy Spirit in our lives.

> I will pray the Father, and he shall give you another Comforter, that he may abide with you for ever; even the Spirit of truth; whom the world cannot receive, because it seeth him not, neither knoweth him: but ye know him; for he dwelleth with you, and shall be in you (John 14:16,17).

This proof will not work for the world because worldly people cannot see the Holy Spirit. But we will understand because He will dwell and work in us.

The word translated "Comforter" in the King James Version of the Bible is "Counselor" in the New International Version and "Advocate" in the New Revised Standard Version. The original Greek word is *Parakletos* (pa-RAH-clay-tos), which we sometimes leave untranslated and call the *Paraclete* (PAIR-uh-cleet). Jesus was speaking of the Holy Spirit, who would come upon them on the Day of Pentecost when "they were all filled with the Holy Ghost, and began to speak with other tongues, as the Spirit gave them utterance" (Acts 2:4). Jesus said that when the disciples would be filled with the Holy Spirit, they would "know that I am in my Father, and ye in me, and I in you" (John 14:20). Those who loved Him and received His Spirit would be loved of His Father, "I will love him, and will manifest myself to him" (John 14:21).

These, then, were Jesus' three proofs of His validity: (1) His own revelation of the Father, (2) answered prayer, and (3) the baptism in the Holy Spirit. These same proofs are needed today to evangelize our communities and our world.

Another Question

The disciples seemed satisfied, but there was one more question. Judas (not Iscariot but the disciple called Lebbaeus or Thaddaeus in other passages) suddenly realized what Jesus was saying. The whole world was wrong, and Jesus was right! That meant the whole world was lost and the only saved people were right there in that conversation! Therefore, Judas asked, "Lord, how is it that thou wilt manifest thyself unto us, and not unto the world?" (John 14:22). Lord, if what You are saying is true, why are we the only ones who know about it? How are we going to get this message out to the world? That is the essential challenge to Christianity and the basic question of missions education in the local church.

Jesus replied to Judas, "If a man love me, he will keep my words: and my Father will love him, and we will come unto him, and make our abode with him . . . . But the Comforter, which is the Holy Ghost, whom the Father will send in my name, he shall teach you all things, and bring all things to your remembrance, whatsoever I have said unto you" (John 14:23,26).

Strategy To Win the World

Jesus' answer about how to get the gospel out to the whole world was centered in the personal experience of His people. First, Jesus would need believers who would love Him and be obedient to Him: "If a man love me, he will keep my words." It all begins with our personal experience with Christ, resulting in our love for Him and obedience to His teachings. He is looking for dedicated, dutiful disciples through whom He may carry out His work. Second, the Trinity—Father, Son, and Holy Ghost—would come and make their abode with the believer.

That was Jesus' answer to how He would get the gospel out to the rest of the world. Did Jesus really answer Judas' question? Shouldn't He have described some sort of program, some organization, some denominational strategy? Shouldn't He have suggested soul-winning classes or seminars on evangelism? Why did He not mention a missiology course on transcultural communication?

Let us not forget that the disciples were already enrolled in the most effective Bible school ever offered to ministers of the gospel—several years of personal apprenticeship with Jesus Christ! We all need all the experience and education we can get; however, here Jesus was dealing at a much more fundamental level. The basic unit of evangelism is the obedient, Christ-loving disciple who believes in Jesus, in miraculous answers to prayer, and in the operation of the Holy Spirit, and in whom dwells the Father, Son, and Holy Spirit. Take any person with those characteristics and set him or her down anywhere on earth, and there will result a growing body of believers who will in turn reproduce themselves by the very life within them.

That was Jesus' plan for world missions, His design for evangelizing the whole world. It was in the light of this strategy that He said in John 20:21, "Peace be unto you: as my Father hath sent me, even so send I you."

The Search for Meaning

It is a most frightening revelation when we realize how few churches are committed to the cause of Christ in the world. Let us go further than that: even in the most missions-oriented churches, many individuals are only minimally involved in reaching out to the world. It is time for a new revival, a new *Pentecostal* revival, for even Jesus said we could not evangelize the world without the active power of the Holy Spirit (John 14:16–26; Acts 1:8).

We need a renewed sense of purpose in the church, a revived sense of meaning, of who we are and what we are supposed to do. Perhaps we need to examine ourselves to see if we really know who we are and what we are about.

Pleasure, Power, and Physical Motivation

Early in this century, Sigmund Freud said people seek pleasure or gratification through whatever makes them feel good. This school of psychology led to the uncontrolled search for pleasure in our times and is at work when Christians fall into physical sins of the flesh.

Another early psychologist, Alfred Adler, disagreed and said people look for power or whatever gives them advantage, authority, or manipulation over others. This supported the American business structure with its competition and its assertive behavior, and the power struggles in families, communities, and committees—or too often in church, district, and national boards.

Carl G. Jung, another early psychologist, said we seek a whole complex set of things depending on our currently perceived need. For instance, a starving man would not seek pleasure or power, but food. Jung's teachings seem to be the closest yet to the Old Testament view of human personality development. This approach to human behavior has not yet come into its own because most of today's psychologists rely on medical cures rather than trying to understand their patients' real problems or seeking cures.

The Most Fundamental Motivation

Viktor E. Frankl, a victim of the Nazi concentration camps at Auschwitz and Dachau and the father of the psychotherapeutic school of logotherapy, went beyond basic biological needs and said that the most fundamental human motive is to find meaning in life. He said that people want a sense of worth and to know that they are fulfilling some significant place in their world. Frankl's observation of our search for meaning generally complements the teachings of Carl Jung yet approaches human behavior from a different viewpoint.

Good News Motivation

If what we are seeking is meaning in life, then the gospel is good news indeed. Through Christ, we know who we are, where we came from, and where we are going. Furthermore, we know what we are supposed to do while we are here.

The very best way to give meaning to the local church is to

involve the congregation in the most urgent claims of Jesus Christ. By committing itself to the task of world evangelization, a church gains a strong sense of its meaning, its place in the world.

Take, for example, the daily human activity of watching television. A member of a missions-involved church sees a news report on a volcanic eruption in the Philippine Islands. She goes to prayer because she knows her church supports missionaries near that area and that churches and believers may be in danger. She asks prayer for the need in her weekly home Bible study and talks with the pastor, who calls the national office and learns that the church's missionary is indeed in the troubled zone. The whole church prays and sends a special offering to help the missionary with his added expenses. Such teamwork occurs when Christians identify themselves with the task of world evangelization and find meaning in missions.

Another Christian sees TV reports of starving children in East Africa and hears the appeals of different agencies seeking help. He feels helpless in the face of such a terrible famine, but wants to do something to help. The newscaster adds that much of the money given for such needs either is spent on administration and fund-raising or never gets to the people in need because of graft, mismanagement, or a lack of interest from local authorities. The Christian wants to help, but he wants his donation to get to the people who need it with a minimum of overhead expense. Because he is a member of a missions-minded church, he is able to send his contribution where it can do the most good for the least cost. In the Assemblies of God, only 5 percent of missionary donations is taken out for its emergency fund; 95 percent goes to the designated project. Many secular or parachurch agencies spend as much as 80 percent of contributions on administration and fund-raising. The Christian is able to do something meaningful and effective through his own missions-involved church.

Even when wars break out, missionaries are often somewhere nearby. Sometimes a U.S. embassy will order Americans out of a dangerous area, and yet we may know that we have national churches and believers in the midst of the conflict zone. We should back them in prayer and prepare to help them when we can get back into their area.

Just knowing that we belong to a church that is doing something significant in the world gives meaning to our Christian lives. Rather than feeling guilty for living in disobedience to Christ, we respond with joy to the missionaries and their ministries. The Assemblies of God is working at some level in more than 130 nations of the world.

It Only Makes Sense

Our involvement in world missions also binds our American churches together with a common bond. One church may have little in common with the style of another church across town, but both support the same missionary and share the same missionary burden for the world. The world-missions cause unites them in purpose, even though they may be socially, culturally, or economically different.

Differences Abound

Have you ever wondered why Pentecostal churches are so different from each other? On one side of town is a community-style church that tries to be nice to everybody, has a friendly worship style, and provides family services. Across town is a bigger church with an impressive music program and frequent big-name speakers that seeks to attract the more influential people in the area. Somewhere near the center is a downtown church that uses drums and tambourines in its worship and tries to reach the ethnically diverse inner city. Then, of course, there is a country-style church with guitars, lots of electronic gadgets, and an informal, chatty style. Yet another Pentecostal church may operate in another language with its own unique songs and pattern to the service.

This diversification of Pentecostal churches confuses some people, and the members of one group may criticize other groups for not being as spiritual as they are. Yet the truth is that

Spirit-filled people have been culturally varied since the Day of Pentecost, when people of different linguistic groups gathered to observe and to participate in the same spiritual experiences. That day 3,000 converts were added to the Church. Each returned to his land to preach the gospel in his own tongue and in the context of his own culture. The variety of Pentecostal churches today only demonstrates the depth to which the Movement is affecting our multilevel, multiracial, multicultural, multieconomic society.

Differences Are Healthy

The diversification of Pentecostal churches is a very healthy sign of the dynamic life in our Movement. If we could just learn to stop criticizing each other for doing things differently than the church across town, we would be even more effective in evangelizing our own communities in depth. Some people will not be evangelized in a setting of moaning pipe organs and whispering congregations; others will not be reached in the raucous atmosphere of drums, tambourines, and shouting praise. And the mediocrity of churches that have no recognizable style will also never win everyone. If the quiet churches would just learn the difference between "conservative" and "dead," if the noisy churches would only discover that it takes more than volume to reach God's throne, and if those middle-of-the-road safe churches would just take some risks and do something daring for the Lord, we might learn to appreciate or at least tolerate one another. Then maybe we could form a stronger bond together to fulfill the Great Commission in our world.

Differences Build Bridges

Our ability to bridge ethnic barriers and express the gospel and our worship in other languages and in a wide variety of cultural patterns is one of the outstanding hallmarks of the Pentecostal movement. We seldom analyze it, but we do it very well. This same characteristic makes us especially effective as missionaries.

What "Missionary" Means

The word *missionary* means different things to different people. Mention it in Ireland, and you'll get into a discussion about St. Patrick, who introduced Christianity and is said to have driven all the snakes from the island. Hawaiians will talk about the early missionaries' insensitivity to their culture in insisting on ankle-length, long-sleeved dresses in the tropics. American Indians will tell you how the early Spanish missionaries enslaved the native populations and killed off whole tribes by malnutrition, mistreatment, and disease. Americans of traditional churches will refer to missionary compounds, orphanages, hospitals, and schools. And they will admire people such as Albert Schweitzer, who gave up a brilliant theological career to build a missionary compound in the heart of Africa—an approach now considered ineffective for missions and damaging to the host culture.

The work of Pentecostal missionaries today has very little in common with what was called "missionary" in the past. Early in the 20th century many missionary organizations built compounds, often with high walls and iron gates, where they brought the native people to teach them English so they could read the King James Bible and receive the gospel. Many missionaries failed to distinguish between Christianization and Westernization. All Christians had to speak and to dress like European or American Christians, and the native people were treated like children. For that reason, that kind of missionary work has been called paternalistic.

Today's successful growth of the Church abroad did not occur until the Pentecostal missionaries came on the scene with their respect for other cultures and their belief that God can work through anyone who is saved and filled with the Holy Spirit. The Pentecostal missionaries emphasized personal experience with Christ and mobilized people with little formal preparation, giving opportunities for service to anyone with a heart for ministry. Combined with the Pentecostal expectation of the soon coming of Jesus Christ, there was a breakdown of the traditional separation between clergy and laypeople as whole congregations were mobilized to share the gospel with everyone within reach. Although this often brought persecution and sometimes martyrdom, it produced an army of fiery-eyed witnesses for Jesus Christ that created the fastest-growing element of the Church in the world.

Ever since the Day of Pentecost when people of 15 different cultures (Acts 2:9–11)[1] saw Christians being blessed and heard the preaching of the gospel, the missionary work of Spirit-filled people has introduced the full gospel to people all over the world and allowed it to grow freely and naturally in the people's own land and culture. We call this principle the indigenous church, the church that grows naturally in its own soil. The people in each country have their own songs played on their own instruments, and gospel literature and Bibles printed in their own language. Some missionaries have dedicated their lives to the preparation and printing of Christian literature; others have painstakingly translated the Bible into local languages—all to provide the necessary materials to the growing national churches. The song services seldom sound like those of Northern Europe or America. The sermons are preached in the local language, and the patterns of worship are unique to the culture being reached, but we are truly going into all the world and preaching the gospel to every creature.

Beyond the indigenous church with its national churches, a greater internationalism is developing in which our Lord will be able to mobilize His forces anywhere for any purpose without regard for nationalistic boundaries or limitations.

By involving ourselves in world missions, we find meaning for our lives and in doing so bring meaning to other lives all around the world.

[1]Parthians, Medes, Elamites, Mesopotamians, Judeans, Cappadocians, Pontians, Asians, Phrygians, Pamphylians, Egyptians, Libyans, Romans, Cretans, and Arabians all heard "them speak in tongues the wonderful works of God"—15 cultures plus the Galilean Christians.

10
Lighting the Flame

Missions is a heart-and-mouth condition! No matter how much we may know about missions, until it affects the heart and mouth we will not spread the gospel, for "out of the abundance of the heart the mouth speaketh" (Matthew 12:34). Missions also affects the vision, the knees, the mind, and the feet.

> How beautiful upon the mountains are the feet of him that bringeth good tidings, that publisheth peace; that bringeth good tidings of good, that publisheth salvation; that saith unto Zion, Thy God reigneth! (Isaiah 52:7).

Do your eyes get a little misty when missionaries speak about the condition of the lost? Do you sometimes wake up in the night and get on your knees to pray for some missionary who has come to your mind? Do you find yourself explaining world events as God's way of shaking loose old traditions and opening new mission fields? Do you have wandering feet that want to leave your place of safety and go to the unsaved, across the backyard fence, across the street, across social or cultural barriers, across American soil, or across borders and oceans?

Then you've caught the vision of missions! And, if you don't isolate yourself quickly, you will spread it to others! You may try to close your mind, shut your mouth, or stop your feet, but you won't succeed because you've caught the vision.

That brings up an important point: a missionary vision may be better caught than taught. Missions education requires exposure to missions itself, not just to an emphasis or teaching on the subject.

Think of a hot-fudge sundae with vanilla ice cream topped with dark chocolate, whipped cream, and nuts, and with a red maraschino cherry pressed artistically into the top. Isn't that a wonderful thought? Can't you just taste the sundae now? Yet the description is not the same as the experience of eating the real thing. We don't want pictures or words about the subject; we want to take a spoon in hand and eat!

It should come as no surprise that children remember best what they experience. Pictures of elephants elicited few comments from a first-grader. However, on returning home from his first visit to a zoo, he could not wait to tell his mother all about the elephants. Using dramatic motions, he showed her how they walked. He swung his arm to demonstrate how they moved their trunks. No amount of information about elephants could have produced the effect of the live elephants themselves.

Snakes and Piranhas

When I was a high school freshman in Spokane, Washington, my pastor father, Alfred R. Womack, invited Missionary Earl Wilke of Bolivia to our church. I had just earned some money shoveling snow for our neighbors and had in my possession my very first $10 bill—a good amount of money in 1948. We lived next door to the church, and naturally I put that bill away before I went to the missionary service.

In those days, one of the standard props of every missionary to the tropics was a big snakeskin. Missionaries were only beginning to use colored slides then. Before slides were available, elaborate foreign paraphernalia would often be displayed.

On this occasion, the missionary called me to the platform and asked if I would help him unroll his snakeskin in front of all the people. The girls in our youth group were all aghast, and the boys frowned because they were jealous. It seemed as if that anaconda skin would unroll forever—at least for 30 feet—and I held the mouth end of that snake for a long time as the missionary talked about the dangers of the Amazonian jungles.

Later, when my father took up the missionary offering, I sat and cried, thinking of the missionary's bravery and feeling guilty for having left my $10 bill in my room. Right after church, I hurried home and came back with the money. I then did what no pastor's child should ever be allowed to do: I got into the offering. I added my $10, which was all the money I had in the world, but I've never been sorry I gave it for missions.

Years later, when I was a missionary to South America, I sat in a jungle hut eating a piranha fish I had caught in the Lengup River. (The fish was bony, but much better than the alternative of being eaten!) I remember thinking about Earl Wilke and his snakeskin and wondered if I should have had that piranha stuffed and mounted to display in my missionary services. In later years, as home secretary for the Assemblies of God Division of Foreign Missions, I raised a lot of missionary money. I probably hold one of the records for the number of missionary services. In the last year of my 13 years in that office, I raised $1 million by direct mail. However, no offering has ever been as important to me as that first $10 when I gave all I had for the cause of Christ. Even though I had an experience in Bible college that I consider my missionary call, I look back to that time when I first participated in a missionary service and put my own money into world missions.

Many of our missionaries can point to similar experiences that awakened their interest in missions at a young age. According to the Division of Foreign Missions, most missionaries first become interested in a missionary career in junior high school. If that is true, we are missing something by putting most of our missions promotion and emphasis on adults.

Let's Play!

We have said that preschool education is based on the concept of play as an educational medium. Actually, that idea is not limited to little children. Isn't that also why adults plan missionary banquets and parades or dress in foreign costumes? Even when teams of men and women travel to a foreign country to help build a church or a Bible school, a big factor in their going is the adventure of the trip. (If you don't believe that, just try to get the same group to help remodel a home-missions church just a few miles away! They might do it, but it wouldn't be as much fun and there wouldn't be as much shopping.)

We can talk about the differences between children and adults, but there's something of the child in all of us. We learn best when we enjoy the experience. We may not agree with much of what Sigmund Freud said about human behavior, but we must agree that we tend to choose pleasure over pain; we choose things we enjoy over things that bore or bother us. In much of our missions education we would be wise to seek methods that people would enjoy while learning about the most serious business in the world.

When a pastor had Missionary Ralph Hiatt of Argentina speak at a midweek service, he asked the Missionettes and Royal Rangers to join the adults in the sanctuary. The leaders were cooperative, but the children were not enthusiastic about sitting with the adults. However, they all came alive and sat on the edge of their seats when Ralph Hiatt brought out his Argentine dummy Felipe and turned out to be an expert ventriloquist. The children learned more from Felipe in the following few minutes than they ever would have from the missionary.

Another missionary, Jerry Smith of Ecuador, made the rounds of the Sunday school classes between morning services. In each class he showed the students a picture of a jungle mother with her cheeks bulged out and holding an undressed child. He asked each group, "What is the mother doing?" Not one person guessed the truth that she was warming the water in her mouth to give her child a bath! This awakened the students' interest and gave the missionary the opportunity to talk about working for God in another culture.

Dress-Up for Missions

Home missionaries working among American Indians learned

long ago to wear feathered war bonnets and beaded leather when attending missions conventions. Who knows how many supporting pastors have been named honorary chiefs? Wearing a war bonnet may be a bit obvious and totally unofficial, but it gets the home missionaries their monthly support.

Missions conventions, district council missionary services, and even the General Council missionary parade often feature missionaries dressed in foreign costumes. Although some such costumes are truly typical, at least of a country's past, they sometimes create confusion rather than increasing the understanding of foreign cultures. Wearing some costumes is a bit like having a visitor to Japan dress in a Nashville "rhinestone cowboy" outfit with chaps and guns to represent the culture of the United States. Yet costumes are fun and sometimes even informative.

For a number of years I had the responsibility of organizing the missionary parades at the Assemblies of God General Councils. On one such occasion, I looked over the crowd of brightly if bizarrely dressed missionaries and spotted a friend with a tasseled black shawl wrapped around him. I said, "You're dressed like a Colombian country woman!"

He grinned and put a finger to his lips, then whispered to me, "Don't tell anybody! I forgot my costume, and this was all we had with us." So, there he was dressed in a woman's costume before the whole General Council!

That same year, another missionary wore a pin-striped business suit with a conservative tie. When asked about his costume, he said, "I'm dressed like a Spanish banker."

A home missionary to the Alaskan Eskimos was in a missions convention in Panama City, Florida. Because it was so hot there, he didn't wear much clothes under his fur parka, fur pants, and fur boots. His costume was impressive, but once on the platform he couldn't take anything off and nearly died of heat exhaustion before the service was over.

The point is that missionary costumes are fun and help us to accept other cultures. A variation on having the missionaries dress in foreign outfits is to have the children, the youth, or even the adults of the church dress for the occasion. Have a world-missions parade with the participants carrying placards of different countries supported by the church and promotion about the various departmental programs.

At the Light–for–the–Lost steak-outs held for many years at First Assembly of God in Los Gatos, California, the men gave prizes for the best cowboy and cowgirl outfits. Everyone came dressed for the occasion. For several years in a row, a Hispanic-American world-missions coordinator from one of the local churches won first prize by coming dressed as a Mexican revolutionary complete with guns and ammunition belts. Everybody enjoyed those dinners, and we raised thousands of dollars for missions.

Enjoyment With a Purpose

It may all be just big kids acting like little kids, but keeping our world-missions vision alive in our congregations can be a lot of fun. It's all right to have fun with the missions programs, as long as behind all the play there is the purpose. We are engaged in the most solemn business in the world, and only because of its deadly seriousness can we afford some comic relief by smiling as we go forth to battle.

Fun for its own sake may lead to a shallow understanding of world missions, but combined with good planning and a well-defined purpose it can be an extremely effective tool for missions education. The entertainment of a missionary parade is only an introduction to a whole program to raise money for missions. After the parade, the congregation sings a missionary hymn, such as "I'll Go Where You Want Me To Go," and the choir may sing "To the Regions Beyond." A missionary brings a fervent challenge, and the pastor collects faith promises. Young people weep at the altar as they seek God's will for their lives. No, it's not all fun and games, but serious people may enjoy their service to the Lord.

Speaking of enjoyment, some of the greatest gospel music ever written has been on the theme of world missions. Nothing will inspire a congregation for missions more than a good choir cantata that encourages believers to go into all the world and preach the gospel to every creature.

Working on the annual missions-convention theme is another enjoyable experience. Each year the Division of Foreign Missions presents a new theme and provides banners, posters, and other materials; however, it's also good once in a while to create your own theme. Name a committee of creative people and watch them get excited about presenting the missionary challenge to the congregation.

Age-Level Missions

In many churches, missions education is limited to the Boys and Girls Missionary Crusade (BGMC) in the Sunday school, Speed–the–Light (STL) in the youth program, Women's and Men's Ministries for adults, and missions conventions and the ministry of visiting missionaries for all the congregation. Although these programs are wonderful, they are not enough to accomplish the whole task. Furthermore, most churches do not coordinate their various programs and emphases with any integrated design. We must create an environment for learning in which missions thinking results from a great variety of influences all coordinated by a single strategic plan.

Early Childhood

For preschool children, we should include in their play environment a variety of educational toys, such as dolls with different skin coloring or dressed in foreign costumes. Some picture books should feature pictures of foreign countries or of missionaries. Life Publishers in Miami puts out a missionary coloring book. Good missionary stories are available from BGMC or probably at your local Bible bookstore. We must create an environment that includes missions.

One church has a monthly session in which the parents join their preschool children by sitting on the floor with them and discussing some mutually important topics. Sometimes they pass around foreign artifacts that the children can touch and explore.

Jesus said, "Suffer [allow] the little children to come unto me, and forbid them not: for of such is the kingdom of God" (Mark 10:14). We must give some thought to what we may be doing that discourages the little children from a full experience and understanding of the purpose of Jesus Christ in their lives. The worst thing we can do is to ignore preschool children, thinking that we can train them later in the ways of world missions. Psychologists say that a large percentage of all the questions we will ever ask in our lives we ask when we are 4 years old. If you don't believe me, just spend a day with one of those little chatterboxes.

Elementary Children

For school-age children the range of missions education is limitless. The emphasis should be on a variety of approaches. By using posters and foreign artifacts we may provide an environment conducive to questions and other involvements. Teachers should talk often about missions and encourage visiting missionaries to come to their classes.

One junior class made a project of finding out all they could about missionary work in Holland. The students wrote to the Division of Foreign Missions for up-to-date information and contacted missionaries to obtain pictures and descriptions of their work. The children researched the history and geography of the country, had their parents make Dutch costumes, and decorated their classroom with windmills, wooden shoes, and plenty of tulips. On a Sunday morning they went before the whole congregation in costume and sang a song in Dutch that they had learned from a tape a missionary had sent them from the Netherlands. After the service, the people came by the junior classroom to see the decorations and to snack on Dutch cheeses. That day the church took up a generous offering to send to Holland for ministries to children.

Such projects for children may take enormous amounts of

time and work, but they are well worth the efforts of the dedicated adults who plan them and carry them out.

YOUTH

For junior high, high school, and college young people many of the same methods apply. These age-groups also require a missions-friendly environment, missionary projects, and the fun of being involved in the missions convention. The national Youth Department has 52 ideas for high interest in missions for youth services and FIRE prayer groups. In addition, young people are particularly susceptible to peer pressure. Being exposed to the teenage children of missionaries is one of the best things that can happen to a church's youth group. Missionaries often do not bring their older children with them on itineration because they are in school, so such contacts should be planned and not left to happenstance. Some larger churches provide furlough housing for missionary families precisely so their congregation will experience living contact with them. Wouldn't it be wonderful if more churches did that? It would bless their people and save thousands of dollars of rent for the grateful missionaries during their months at home.

Fire, Smoke, or Ashes?

Many missionaries make their key choices after they have become adults. Some are converted during overseas military service; they come home to get their preparation and return to a missionary career. Others sense their calling during their Bible college years. However, the majority of missionaries testify that God began to call them at an early age. If this is true, then how early should we expect to see future missionaries begin to carry out their calling?

As a young child in Nazareth, Jesus "grew, and waxed strong in spirit, filled with wisdom; and the grace of God was upon him" (Luke 2:40). That would have been during His preschool, primary, and junior years if He had lived in our culture. At 12 years old, He said, "I must be about my Father's business"

(Luke 2:49). If in Jesus' early life we see the beginning of ministry that was to be revealed in its fullness many years later, should we not expect to see similar progress in boys and girls upon whom God has placed His hand today?

As we carry out missions education in the local church, we must remain aware that we may be fostering young missionaries who will someday bear the burden of world evangelization. How should we treat them, and what should we do to train them?

The Right Kind of Church

If we are going to depend on such missionaries to preach and teach the gospel, win converts to Jesus Christ, lead people into the fullness of the baptism in the Holy Spirit, and accompany their ministries with signs and wonders of divine healing and deliverance, then they deserve to grow up in churches where they will learn such things at an early age. One of the most important things a church can do for missions education is to be the kind of church in America that we want our missionaries to raise up on the foreign fields.

In Mark 16:17,18, Jesus said, "These signs shall follow them that believe"—the casting out of devils, speaking in tongues, deliverance from threats in nature, deliverance from human threats, and divine healing. These signs were to be seen in every church of Christian believers. Jesus gave that promise to people to whom He had just said, "Go ye into all the world, and preach the gospel to every creature" (Mark 16:15). If we believe such things will happen for missionaries on foreign fields, then we must also expect to experience them in the "sending" churches in America. That is, signs and wonders must be a part of the ministry of all churches in America and abroad.

Seeking Convert Growth

We also should assume that churches that produce future

missionaries will be evangelistic in attitude and action. Here we must distinguish between convert growth and transfer growth. Some people seem to be playing musical churches as they move about from one church to another. With a floating congregation that attends whichever church is currently able to capture its fleeting attention, a church may show signs of growth without actually winning new converts to Christ. The rise of one church will coincide with the decline of another. On a mission field, missionaries do not favor one of their churches over another because they are seeking to increase the total number of converts! Young missionaries need an atmosphere of convert growth in which they themselves will be brought into personal experience with Christ and will regularly observe other people coming to Christ for salvation.

Deep Commitment and Passion for Souls

Young people need to develop within a youth group that is committed to Jesus Christ, is evangelistic, and is on fire for God. They need the kind of youth group where young people go to youth camps, participate in street witnessing, and sit on the front pews of their church.

The Right Training

Young people need to get their ministerial preparation in a Pentecostal Bible college and expect that it, too, will be a center of spirituality and evangelism. And when they graduate and enter the ministry, they deserve to gain their pastoral experience in fully Pentecostal churches whose very life in the Spirit trains them for overseas evangelism. And they deserve to develop their ministries in a Pentecostal movement that remains true to the forces and faith that brought it into being in the first place.

The missions education that we do by explanation may not be nearly as important as that which we do by example.

Holy Ghost Revival

The Pentecostal movement was born in the fire of a Holy

Ghost revival. Like the early and latter rains that fell on the Holy Land in ancient times, so the outpouring of the Holy Spirit that first awakened the Church on the Day of Pentecost fell on believers again on January 1, 1901, at Topeka, Kansas. Bible college students who could not afford to go home for the Christmas holiday had decided to dedicate themselves in one accord to 10 days of prayer and supplication, just as the Lord's first followers did in A.D. 30. On the first day of 1901, the Holy Spirit fell on the students as He had on the Lord's first church on the Day of Pentecost, and "they were all filled with the Holy Ghost, and began to speak with other tongues, as the Spirit gave them utterance" (Acts 2:4).

The revival soon spread to Kansas City, and from there to Texas, California, and out to the whole world. The 1906 Azusa Street Revival in Los Angeles became like a rocket launching pad to send out missionaries to many countries. So many of the new Pentecostal churches began to support missionaries that the need to coordinate their efforts became a major reason for calling a meeting at Hot Springs, Arkansas, in April 1914. There the Assemblies of God was formed, and the revival continued through an organized, coordinated international ministry that has produced the fastest-growing major church in the world. Our Pentecostal forefathers called for "the greatest evangelism that the world has ever seen" (Minutes of the Second General Council, November 1914).

It became popular in the 1940s and 1950s for preachers to say, "I was born in the fire, and the smoke of these dying embers keeps burning my eyes." They were trying to tell us that something was slowing down, becoming less fervent, and adapting to a Pentecostal style without Pentecostal power. They weren't altogether right, for there were powerful churches in those days, as there still are today. Yet, a growing number of churches seldom experienced the supernatural and seemed more adapted to the ways of this world than to reaching the world for Christ. If those preachers were concerned about the smoke of dying embers 40 to 50 years ago, what would they say in some places today in the cold, gray ashes of a long-dead fire?

A missionary who had just finished his year of itineration was asked about the spiritual state of the churches he had visited. He had held nearly 200 missionary services that year, and not once had he heard a single message in tongues and interpretation. Missionaries returning from the fervor of foreign revivals are often shocked at the low-key, laid-back, and apparently lethargic condition of many of the churches in which they minister in America.

Has the Pentecostal fire gone out? Certainly not! There are still many on-fire, all-out, full-gospel churches that are as dedicated to original New Testament Christianity as any churches in the past. Since the latter-day outpouring of the Holy Spirit, there have always been revived and dead churches, representing the whole scope from fiery hot to icy cold with the majority in the uncommitted middle range of cautious lukewarmness. God has already told us what He thinks of that condition: "So then because thou art lukewarm, and neither cold nor hot, I will spew thee out of my mouth" (Revelation 3:16). The meaning is obvious; lukewarm churches make God sick! They will not be a factor in world evangelization.

The answer is to repent, restore, and return. Repent of our cooling down, restore a Pentecostal style to the church, and return to the fire that first set our missionaries aflame with their fervor for world evangelization.

Fire has never changed. It is as effective as it ever was and is unaltered by modern means or technologies. About all you can do with fire is to fan it, fuel it, or put it out. T. C. Cunningham, who for many years was the world-missions director of the Southern California District and a major force in world evangelization, was heard to say, "Some churches are so dry they constitute a fire hazard!" If that is true, somebody strike the match!

If we are to spread the flame of the gospel around the world through our missionaries, we must first possess that fire in our own churches. How, then, may a church light that revival fire?

SEVEN STRATEGIES

1. *Preach more fervently.* This gospel of the Kingdom is too important to be expressed in quiet tones and controlled emotion. We must do what it says in the hymn "Jesus Saves":

> Shout salvation full and free;
> Highest hills and deepest caves;
> This our song of victory,
> Jesus saves! Jesus saves![1]

2. *Worship more energetically.* We used to say, "You get out of a service what you put into it." We were wrong. You always get back more from God than you give, but still it is true that little happens if people do not come to church expecting to hear from God and ready to praise the Lord wholeheartedly and without reservation.

3. *Pray more enthusiastically.* People often are very somber about prayer, even though the Bible says, "Enter into his gates with thanksgiving, and into his courts with praise: be thankful unto him, and bless his name" (Psalm 100:4). In preparation for the Day of Pentecost, the first believers were "with one accord in prayer and supplication" (Acts 1:14). Prayer is expressed in words, but supplication must be expressed from the depth of the soul.

4. *Emphasize the Sunday night service.* Pentecostal worship requires an unlimited opportunity for seeking God at the altar. Generally this cannot happen after a Sunday morning service or after a midweek service shared with Missionettes and Royal Rangers. There are very few strongly Pentecostal churches that do not have an active Sunday night service.

5. *Give priority to revival.* Preach often on the need for it. Promote themes such as "Revival Is Survival!" Invite evangelists for special meetings with a revival emphasis.

6. *Upgrade your music.* Slow, mournful tunes are inconsistent with the reality of God, so think well about the purpose of each service and plan the music accordingly. Pentecost thrives in an atmosphere of joy.

7. *Come together in one accord.* If all the people are determined to have a Pentecostal church and will seek God with all their hearts, God will respond from heaven with an outpouring of the Holy Spirit as He did at Pentecost.

The Pentecostal movement is on the verge of some wonderful days of world evangelization if we can maintain the kind of character that got us where we are today.

A Global Vision; Local Action

Yes, all our churches need to integrate their missions program as a single and pervasive element of their whole program, to give careful attention to missions education, and to convert their local church into a worldwide church with a global vision. The most effective missions-education method is to provide a Pentecostal atmosphere in which the Holy Spirit can do His full work in the lives of everyone in the congregation, influence future missionaries and missions supporters, and send missionaries to the ends of the earth.

In Burkina Faso, West Africa, the Mossi tribesmen on the southern edge of the Sahara Desert prepare for their brief rainy season by burning off all the old dried grass of the longer dry time. They grasp a handful of dry grass in their hands and set fire to it, and then they walk across the land shaking the burning grass and letting the fire fall. Wherever the fire falls, other fires break out until the whole countryside is set aflame.

> Oh, God, look upon our dryness after a long, hot summer without the rain, and let Your fire fall once again! Let young missionaries grow up in Pentecostal churches and go to the ends of the earth to spread the flame that first burned in their hearts in their home churches in America.

---

[1]*Hymns of Glorious Praise* (Springfield, Mo.: Gospel Publishing House, 1969), 171.